TO MY CHILDREN, KIERSTYN AND RYAN

I love you more than anything in this world, even ministry. You are my real passion and my greatest joy is being your Dad.

UNTHINKABLE

A FIELD GUIDE FOR OUTRAGEOUS FAITH

BY RODNEY W. WARDWELL II

UNTHINKABLE

Cover design by Kindred Creative | Kindredcreative.com

ISBN 9798467847481
Printed in the United States of America
2021 – First Edition

TABLE OF CONTENTS

ENDORSEMENTS

"The book *Unthinkable* is more than just one person's manifesto, but it's also the kind of life that God has for you as well. Think of this book as a tool to help you live out your life with great faith. But don't just read it! I want to encourage you to lean into the words of this book. Don't just read through it but pray through it. Don't just read through it but practice the principles you are reading. And when you do, I think you will be surprised that the God who made you will begin to reveal the *unthinkable* plan and purpose that He has for you."

MARK BATTERSON
Lead Pastor of National Community Church and author of New York Times Bestseller, "**The Circle Maker**"

"God has an incredible way of helping you build a platform for your life so that you can make a difference in the lives of others. I've experienced it in my life, and you can in yours as well! The book *Unthinkable* is the beginning of a movement of people who want to live their lives with purpose. I'm on board, and there's room for you. You will not regret it! "

JUSTIN WREN
UFC Fighter and author of "**Fight for the Forgotten**"

In this book, my friend Rodney will have you laughing one minute while having you feel challenged in the next! And the best part is that he practices and lives out what he has written – and what's written in these pages aren't just good ideas, but they are God ideas. So, dive in and become a part of this *unthinkable* movement. It doesn't matter what season you are at on your journey. I know that this book will be one that will forever shape your life.

SCOTT WILSON
CEO of Ready Set Grow and author of "**Impact: Releasing the Power of Influence**"

Rodney is the guy who is always taking on the toughest missions from God. I love this guy. He's not afraid to scale the cliffs that God puts in front of him—which is why he knows how to travel light and keep his soul in sync with God. Throughout *Unthinkable*, Rodney will inspire you with dozens of tools you'll need along the way. With each chapter, Rodney will break off each of the chains that are holding you back from the next level. And get ready: Rodney is a master encourager. This book will pump you up and make you jump out of the airplane into God's great calling on your life!

PETER HAAS
Lead Pastor of Substance Church, author and songwriter for Substance Variant

ENDORSEMENTS

In the book, *Unthinkable*, Rodney challenges us to dream big and to follow the voice of God with our lives. He gives insightful principles to follow that will help you impact the people around you. This book will help you live your life in such a way that when it's all over, you'll have no regrets!

HERBERT COOPER
Senior Pastor at People's Church and author of **"But God Changes Everything"**

In *Unthinkable*, Rodney invites us to go to previously unimaginable places as followers of Jesus. His writing is both invigorating and intriguing as he presents a case for living with fearless faith. I believe this book will be a tool that unearths treasures in your life, community and church. Get ready to grow.

JEFFERY PORTMANN
Director of Church Multiplication Network, Assemblies of God US

If you are looking for a book to move you off the couch and into an adventure, THIS IS IT! Thank you, Rodney, for doing the *unthinkable* and inspiring us to live a story that is worth telling.

WES DAVIS
Lead Pastor of newlife.tv and author of **"People Becoming the Church"**

A faith with no limits. Living out our unspoken dreams and visions we simply don't have the courage to share out loud. Finding ourselves playing defense when we know we are called to play offense. We all want to live a life like this! But for so many of us it feels so...*unthinkable*. Rodney Wardwell compellingly shares his own journey of learning to embrace the *unthinkable* Jesus of the gospels and how we can do the same. Lean into this book!

DAN SERDAHL
Stadia Catalyst and Jedi Master of Networking

INTRODUCTION · INTRODUCTION · INTRODUCTION · INTRODUCTION · INTRODUCTION · INTRODUCTION

Do you remember a time when you believed you could do anything you wanted to? Come on...think back on some of the earliest years of your life. Remember when you would put on your Superman pajamas, tie a blanket around your neck as a cape, and literally thought you could fly? Or what about when you put on a crown and fancy shoes, and twirled around in circles till you were too dizzy to stand? Because you were a princess, you dreamed your knight in shining armor was coming on his horse to whisk you off into the sunset!

Do you remember those days? Do you remember that childlike faith you had – a faith without any limitations? Where did it go? Why did you stop believing?

Ephesians 3:20 tells us that our God is able to do, "immeasurably more than all we ask or imagine."[1] One translation says that God is capable of doing, "more than we might ask or think".[2] In other words, God is the author of the **unthinkable**. Have you ever stopped to grasp what that really means? Take your greatest imaginations and multiply them by ten to the trillionth power and even that amount of imagining is not vast enough. It is, in fact, exponential! Take your ability to dream, now realize what God can do reaches beyond our capacity for that. God is the God of making the impossible become possible. As His sons and daughters, He desires for us to live believing He can accomplish the *unthinkable*. This is not just in our lives…but through our lives. I promise, you can never out-dream the Dreamer!

SO QUIT PLAYING IT SAFE!

It appears to me that many believers have resorted to playing "not to lose" rather than playing to win. I don't know about you, but I would rather not be stuck playing all-time defense. When playing football in the yard, it saddens me to admit that I have reached the age of being the all-time quarterback. It's the day that every young man dreads. As a middle-aged man, I'm in one of the best places health-wise that I have been, but it is the recovery time and what my muscles do to me the following day that have led to my new all-time position. My point is, no one can constantly run the routes and play defense forever, but unfortunately that is where many people find themselves regarding their faith.

Listen, God has not called us to receive His forgiveness only to spend the rest of our lives trying to hold onto and preserve it. Once we receive it, we have been set free. Now it is time to live life on the edge, fulfilling our purpose because Christ didn't come to condemn us, but to set us free. In His freedom, we have everything to gain and nothing to lose!

It's time to start living by faith and believing God for some really big things – it is time to begin living the *unthinkable*!

AND that's what this book is all about.

Throughout the pages of **Unthinkable**, I want to challenge your heart to come into alignment with your faith. We will look at several components of our walk with God and we are going to be challenged to live with an incredible faith in each one of these areas. I am praying that as we go through this together that you will discover a greater boldness in your relationship with Jesus unlike any you have ever experienced before.

So, who exactly is this book for? It is for the schoolteacher, the lawyer, the air traffic controller, the computer professional, the college student, the church planter, the missionary, the barista, the seasoned pastor, and the new believer. It is for those who desire to take the next step with Jesus in their faith. This book is for someone not content to sit back and let life pass them by; it is for those who dare to live boldly for God and desire to begin learning what steps they might take.

God is giving you permission to do the **unthinkable** with your life. In fact, it is the way you were designed and the reason you were created!

Now, when I say God desires to do the **unthinkable** in our lives, I am not promoting throwing caution to the wind, and becoming negligent or ridiculous. I am not suggesting we stand on a box in the middle of Times Square proclaiming the end of the world with our megaphone in one hand and our Bible in the other! That's a bit much and also a little tacky. However, what I *am* saying is that I truly believe, as children of the living God, we need to start stepping out in faith and choose to live an unmistakably passionate life for Jesus. We need to begin believing God for things this world says are absolutely **unthinkable**!

Living the **unthinkable**, finding the path towards a deeper relationship with God and then displaying it to the world around you – that is why I wrote this book, and why you have it in your hands today. I pray you picked up this book because this same thought resonates in your heart. You see, I believe that God wants to use you, to rise up and live for Him in a way that is visible for the whole world to see. You and I need to become people who will not be held back but will dare to do something **unthinkable** in hopes that people will see our faith and be drawn to our God.

So now, let me take a minute and introduce you to someone whose story plays a key role as we move forward.

As a kid, I often heard the story in chapter 19 of the Gospel of Luke. A familiar story to anyone who grew up in church that has become almost commonplace to us. You might recall a clever tune we sang to help remember the story.

> *Zacchaeus was a wee little man*
> *And a wee little man was he*
> *He climbed up in the sycamore tree*
> *For the Lord he wanted to see*
>
> *And when the Savior passed that way*
> *He looked up in the tree*
> *And said, "Zacchaeus, you come down!*
> *For I'm going to your house today!*
> *For I'm going to your house today!*[3]

Due to the nature of children's songs, the tale has lost some of its punch. However, the story is truly a powerful account and is one that we are going to dig into throughout the duration of this book. As we look at the story, allow me to introduce you to a guy who changed my life. Meet my friend, Zac.

> *Jesus entered Jericho and was passing through. A man was there by the name of Zacchaeus; he was a chief tax collector and was wealthy. He wanted to see who Jesus was, but because he was short he could not see over the crowd. So he ran ahead and climbed a sycamore-fig tree to see him, since Jesus was coming that way.*
>
> *When Jesus reached the spot, he looked up and said to him, "Zacchaeus, come down immediately. I must stay at your house today." So he came down at once and welcomed him gladly. All the people saw this and began to mutter, "He has gone to be the guest of a sinner."*
>
> *But Zacchaeus stood up and said to the Lord, "Look, Lord! Here and now I give half of my possessions to the poor, and if I have cheated anybody out of anything, I will pay back four times the amount."*
>
> *Jesus said to him, "Today salvation has come to this house, because this man, too, is a son of Abraham. For the Son of Man came to seek and to save the lost."[4]*

In the chapters ahead, we are going to dive a little bit deeper into Zacchaeus' incredible story and let his actions speak into our lives and teach us how to do the *unthinkable*.

If you will let him, I believe that as you read this book, God is going to teach you how to live out your life with an incredible faith. As believers we cannot afford to sit back and wait any longer.

I encourage you to check out the main ideas and take-away questions at the end of each chapter. Find someone to read this book with that will help you process these questions and ideas. Be careful to read with intention, not zipping through this book without letting each chapter settle into your heart. If you take a few extra minutes at the end of each chapter, I think this book will become a valuable resource for you.

Well, it is time to dive into the first chapter. I personally want to welcome you to the journey! There is nothing better than going after God's best for your life. We are going to have a lot of fun together.

-RODNEY

PART ONE

GOD IS THE AUTHOR OF THE

UN
THINK
ABLE

CHAPTER ONE · CHAPTER ONE · CHAPTER ONE · CHAPTER ONE · CHAPTER ONE · CHAPTER ONE · CHAPTER ONE · CHAPTER ONE

DO HARD THINGS

love adventure. Since childhood, I have not been able to sit still. It drove my parents crazy. At times, I felt like the poster child for ADHD. Well, maybe I was not that bad, but I have always loved to be where the action is!

I will never forget a memory that my parents share about the young, adventurous me. I was a little boy, just two or three years old at the time and my dad played competitive fast pitch softball for the local UAW 977. My parents made these games a family outing each time dad had one. One summer day, we were at Matter Park in my hometown of Marion, Indiana. Mom sat watching the action from the bleachers, while my older brother busied himself as the batboy. I plopped myself down in the sand pile by the bleachers, my pail and shovel by my side as I was ready to make mud pies. Well, the softball game was intense that day. The game was so intense and engaging that no one noticed a three-year-old boy get up from his sand pile and wander away. As you might imagine, as soon as my mother realized that I had disappeared, she began to panic.

Now one detail that I failed to mention is that Matter Park had a large, snake-infested pond as well as an Olympic-sized pool. So, playing out in my mother's head were all the worst-case scenarios that could possibly happen to her little boy. All she could think about was finding and making sure that me, her toe-head, blonde, little boy was found safe.

The softball game was called to a halt as a search party formed and everyone began looking for me. That's right, I shut down an entire softball game!

In a matter of minutes, everyone was able to breathe a sigh of relief when a woman yelled, "Karol," (my mother's name), "he's over here." Where was I, you ask? Well, just on the other side of the park, there was a covered pavilion with a large family reunion gathered and there I was, blending in with that family eating chicken wings and drinking Kool Aid. Can you blame me? Food, it seems has always had that effect on me, though the irresistible scent of chicken never again led me to give my mother such a scare as I did that day.

What can I say? I love adventure! I always have. That love was ingrained in me as an energetic boy exploring my parents five acres of woods in north central Indiana. The dream playground of most every young boy, I could do anything imaginable so long as I was home by dinnertime. Kids these days just don't understand what fun it is to play in nature away from electronic devices and to be able to create your own kingdoms. Ahh, the freedom!

I spent countless hours of my childhood climbing large trees, building forts, and fighting imaginary bad guys (and winning of course). My adventures in those woods are still some of my fondest memories!

As I grew into adulthood, not much changed. The thrill of the new still excites me. My love of adventure has only grown, as I see more and more of the world God created. When I passed into my 40's, I found myself still loving adventure. In fact, I think I may be an adrenaline junkie, a thrill seeker, a real bona fide dreamer!

I love doing hard things and challenging myself to take on adventures that most people would never dare attempt. Things like…

…distance cycling.

…competing in sprint triathlons.

…running marathons.

…and climbing mountains.

In fact, as I sit writing this particular part of the book, I am flying at approximately 40,000 feet over the Rocky Mountains on my way to coach at a church planter training and I can't help but think, "Man, I wish I could climb a few of those 'fourteeners' that I see out the window of this plane."

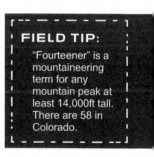

FIELD TIP:

"Fourteener" is a mountaineering term for any mountain peak at least 14,000ft tall. There are 58 in Colorado.

I just love doing exciting things that challenge me and push me to my limits – things that cause me to prepare like I have never prepared before. Here's a truth that I have come to learn and actually live by:

SOMETIMES, IN LIFE YOU JUST HAVE TO DO HARD THINGS!

AND let's face it, so often today we settle for what is easy. Often, we give up just before we experience a break-through.

Look at Zacchaeus in the book of Luke, we're going to be talking a lot about him in future chapters. It would have been easy for him to view his obstacles and give up. He could have easily used his short stature as an excuse. As a dignified tax-collector he could have buckled under the pressure of people's perception of him, a grown man up in a tree. After all, it would have been difficult for him to climb a tree in sandals and a robe, right? Did he fear that people would be able to look right up his man dress and see his undergarments? He could have let all of that hinder him from doing something hard, but he did not. Instead, he chose to set his fears and reservations aside and climb the tree, because more than anything, he wanted to see Jesus. He chose to do the hard thing.

Most of us, on our average day, can do the easy stuff, but God is calling you and I to do something that requires forethought, determination, planning – in other words, he wants us to be intentional. He desires our commitment to do hard things because it is in the struggle of the hard moments and how we handle them that we are defined and that ultimately gives God the glory. It all really comes down to our daily choices. It has been said that choices are the only things we make in life, that eventually come back around and make us. Your choices are shaping who you become, and they profoundly influence your faith.

That is expressly why I want to challenge you to take your faith to a different level by changing your mindset. Determine in your heart to move beyond what *is* and embrace the struggle of attempting to do the *right things*, even when they are the *hard things*.

The following is an excerpt from my climbing journal, and I'll be sharing some entries with you throughout this book...

KILIMANJARO, THE ROOFTOP OVER AFRICA
MONDAY, SEPTEMBER 16TH, 2013

Today, we set out for our adventure. After staying up until midnight getting all our gear packed, we finally fell asleep. We woke up, enjoyed some breakfast at the hotel when a man named Evans showed up to take us in his van to Moshi [in Tanzania]. Nate and I were both excited to get there and we were glad to finally arrive and meet Rodin, our climbing guide. He was young, vibrant, and he had a good grasp on English and our American culture knowing some slang. Some that was fun and some that I would be too embarrassed to repeat. I'm not sure he fully understood what he was saying, either.

Well, we arrived at Machame Gate very excited. Like most good things, we had to wait a while to begin. I was surprised to see so many nationalities. After signing the "Climber's Registration Book" at the gate, we grabbed our packs (our overnight equipment went with the porters), and we walked through the gate and began towards the first night's stop - Machame Camp.

The trail was a good four-hour-hike, and it was as if we were walking through a forest the entire time. The pathways were pads of dirt and tree stumps the entire way. By the end of the day, we had reached 3,000 meters above sea level or 9,750 feet.

All in all, we were acclimating well to the altitude changes and the scenery was awesome. We signed in the book at the new camp while the porters set up camp for us. We found that we had our own port-a-pot, something that is a luxury item and not always the norm.

Tonight, they fed us cucumber soup and fried fish. It was actually pretty good. We are going to bed around 7pm since the sun sets so early due to the fact that Tanzania is so close to the equator. I'm excited and ready to get going again in the morning!

Now, when you tell people in the United States that you are going to fly to another continent to climb a mountain, they look at you as if you are crazy. Well, for me it all began as a passing comment that dates all the way back to November of 2010 in Tulsa, Oklahoma.

As a student pastor one of my greatest passions was teaching students how to give big and live generously. In fact, it's one of the core values of the church I pastor today and a key to **unthinkable** living. I have always wanted to lead the charge by example. In the years leading up to this particular day, I had previously ridden my bicycle across both Kansas and Oklahoma on separate occasions raising money for missions.

So, on this beautiful Sunday morning in November, I set out to run my very first full marathon. All 26.2 grueling miles! It truly was an incredible accomplishment, and I was blessed to have an awesome team of people come to cheer me on.

However, as I crossed the finish line and began the cool down process I was wiped out. As I climbed into the passenger seat of the car for the journey back home, I said to one of my friends, Nathan, "Well, I've ridden my bike across the state, I've completed a marathon for missions, what's next?" Then I smiled and I said, "I guess I'll have to go climb a mountain."

And I still believe to this day that something as crazy as that slipped out of my mouth for the first time in passing, and what felt like just a funny comment to my friend, became so much more. Today I believe, and what I didn't fully realize then, was that as I said those words a seed was being planted in my heart. And it would be something over time I simply couldn't shake.

Yes, I had a lot of questions to answer and a lot of doubts and concerns. But often God just wants to know if you are willing to go on the journey and go along for the ride if you are crazy enough to even speak it out loud for other people to hear. At least that's the way it has been for me.

I have discovered that the more God talks to me about something, the more I have to talk about it to other people. Eventually that vision and that idea become planted so deep in my heart that I am unable to get away from it. It seems like a pipe dream with a whole lot of questions and blanks still to be filled in. But in the end, the Lord takes care of all the details, and actually, discovering the details is one of the most exciting parts of the process. (We'll talk about this further in the upcoming chapters!)

However, what we have to understand is that contrary to what our culture has taught us, God isn't always calling us to take the path of least resistance. Sometimes there will be two choices and the one that seems like the obvious option because it is the easiest, is not always the direction that God is calling us to go.

YOUR CHOICES ARE SHAPING WHO YOU WANT TO BECOME

Many times God leads us to the most challenging path, a path that is riddled with all sorts of headaches. As the old adage from Thomas Jefferson says, "With great risk comes great reward,"[1] but often there's more to it because it can also come with great resistance. It comes with the territory. So, you and I, we just have to learn to lower our head and lean into the storm.

One thing I have noticed is that when a new trail has been blazed, it didn't emerge without someone having to pull out the machete and clear away the brush. New pathways are almost always responsible for bruised shins and cut up legs for those who have cleared them out. It takes work. Hard work!

Sure, doing hard things will challenge you to your core, but it's the burden behind it that God has given you that will drive you to the bitter end. Can't stop, won't stop!

Again, I'm no stranger to hard things and honestly, I find enjoyment and fulfillment in doing and accomplishing hard things. But here's what I want you to know, you don't have to be wired like I am to still step out and do hard things. You might never even think twice about skydiving. The thought of running a marathon or climbing a mountain might absolutely scare you to death. But I want you to know that you are still a prime candidate to do the *unthinkable* with your life! A little later in this book, I'm going to share with you some ways that you can do just that.

But first, I think it's time that I let you in on one of the most *unthinkable* things I have ever been a part of. Something that today I am so absolutely passionate about! So go ahead and walk through and talk out the review questions to chapter one with a group of friends, your small group, or chew on them by yourself, and then turn over to chapter two so I can tell you all about it.

FIELD NOTES

KEY IDEAS:

- Choices are the only thing in life that we make that come back around and eventually make us.
- Choose to do the right thing even when it is the hard thing!
- The burden that God gave you will be the driving force to keep you going!

FOLLOW-UP QUESTIONS:

1. What is it that is causing you to want to play it safe with your life? Fear? Anxiety? The unknown? What can you do to help yourself overcome that hesitancy?
2. Have you ever said something in passing and then after thinking over it for a while you realize that what you said might have some truth and value to it – that maybe as crazy as it was, it was a God thought or idea?
3. What are some of the hard things that God is calling you to do right now?

FIELD
NOTES

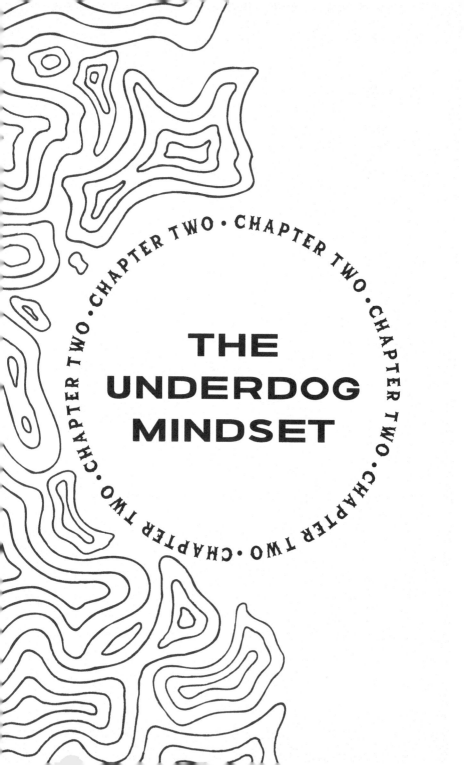

THE UNDERDOG MINDSET

After graduating from Central Bible College in the spring of 2002, my wife Kate and I stepped into full-time student ministry. We were just two early twenty-somethings who met in college, fell in love, and wanted to invest in the next generation. Neither one of us had grown up in a ministry family. Our parents were not pastors. We were simply two people who loved doing life with and ministering to students.

To put it plainly, I think we always felt like underdogs. For those of you unfamiliar with the term, someone is an underdog when the odds are stacked against them; meaning they are not expected to win. Yet that is exactly how we felt in comparison to many of our friends who appeared to know ministry inside and out. They had family legacies within ministry and generations of leaders in their lineage.

Interestingly, we still had enough faith to keep believing that we stood a chance, despite where our family tree seemed lacking. We knew in our hearts that God had called us to accomplish something special and we had read enough scripture to know that God often chooses and champions underdogs!

I want to tell you about our biggest **unthinkable** moment, but before that I feel I should mention we began green and naïve in ministry. After serving for a combined 13½ years in three different areas of the church, student ministry became a comfortable place for us. We had grown to love the ministry we were involved in, and by all standards had become quite good at it, too.

Over this period of time, we were able to participate in two major building projects. We helped students raise more than $150,000 for world mission's projects. We saw hundreds of students come to faith in Christ and sent dozens to places of ministry training. We absolutely loved what we were doing, and honestly, never envisioned ourselves doing anything different.

Nevertheless, God began to birth something new in our hearts and the words church planting started coming up in our conversations.

ALL IT TAKES IS A DETER MINA TION TO KEEP CLIMBING

Church planting had never been a desire in our lives before. On one occasion, while traveling, I ran into my friend Herbert Cooper. I was on a scouting trip to the Dominican Republic for a missions' trip planned later that summer, and he was boarding a plane for Arizona to speak at a church planting conference. I was excited for the opportunity to put things in motion for my students and leaders who I would be bringing back to the

Dominican Republic, and I had high hopes for the trip. Herbert had just planted a thriving church in Edmond, Oklahoma. We only talked briefly, but I will never forget something that he said. Herbert had just come off the evangelistic field a few years earlier to plant People's Church. So, I asked him how the church was and what the transition was like. He replied, "I'm loving every minute of it. Church planting is the extreme sport of pastoring."

I vividly recall that conversation and ironically, my internal response was, "I'm so glad it's you, Herbert, and not me. Absolutely not."

You know how it is, in any field, you see the people in senior leadership around you and you try to imagine yourself there. Kate and I were still young, and we did not see ourselves as the people who would become the lead pastors of a church. We looked at ourselves and tried to determine whether we fit the mold or not. In our minds, no one over twenty-five would have wanted to follow *us* as their lead pastors. Part of that realization was insecurity but there were facts too. We lived in rural Midwest America. I had a mohawk, and Kate played the electric guitar and did not cook or do crafts. We just did not feel like we were the prime candidates to lead a church.

Often what God calls us to do, are things we never imagined for our lives or even envisioned ourselves attempting. When we decided to lead a church planting team, we knew it was due to the prompting and the work of the Lord, who was calling us to start a new church in Oklahoma City. That encouragement from the Holy Spirit is why I also felt so compelled to write this book.

BACK TO ZAC

Remember our friend Zacchaeus? Now here is a man who did the **unthinkable** with his life. Picture it with me; there is a rising hum and buzz coming from outside of the city gates. A man by the name of Jesus has decided to make His way to town.

The way people are talking, this Jesus has really generated a following. Stories are being told of the things He has done. Some people are calling them *miracles*.

Not long ago, while Jesus was speaking at the house of a follower, a few men cut a hole in the roof and lowered a mat down with the crippled body of their friend; dropping him in front of Jesus as He was teaching. Suddenly, a hush fell among the people. No one could believe their eyes. What were they seeing and what was Jesus going to say?

Everyone was perplexed at His response. Most people would have been upset to be interrupted, but not Jesus. Not only was He unphased by the interruption, but what He did next was absolutely **unthinkable** – Jesus stretched His hand out towards the lame man and healed him.[1]

That is only one of the stories. There are so many more. Stories of the blind regaining sight, food being multiplied enough to feed thousands, and of those who were dead but being brought back to life when Jesus intervened.

So, when Zacchaeus heard that this man was coming to town, he too was intrigued and wanted to see Him.

Zacchaeus had a certain stature that in his culture, pointedly made him an underdog. We are told he was a bit "vertically challenged". As you can imagine, when the crowds intensified and grew, Zacchaeus' visibility dwindled. As people packed the streets, it became increasingly difficult to view Jesus as He came down the road in Jericho.

If you have ever attended a parade, then you too have probably experienced this uncomfortable feeling. The convergence of people coming together naturally creates the need for a better vantage point. That is why we see children riding on shoulders at events like these. Those lucky few that arrive early to the parade get the best seats along the curb where they can run out and pocket the candy thrown to the crowd.

As a kid, I was a late bloomer. I was small all the way until the summer of my sophomore year of high school. It wasn't until then that I hit a nine-inch growth spurt. I understood this feeling of being short all too well.

So, Zacchaeus was out of luck, right? Or was he? I love that Zac had a fight inside of him, that he kept at it and never gave up. When some might have thrown in the towel, he got creative and innovative. Zacchaeus wanted to get a glimpse of this miracle maker, this Jesus. Nothing was going to stop him. In his culture, he was certainly an underdog, but no one bothered to tell him he was supposed to lose. So, I picture it like this: He cinched up his robe, pulled it around in such a way that he could remain decent, bent down, and pumped up his sandals like a sick 90's Reebok commercial, and he began his ascent to the top of a nearby sycamore tree. All so he could catch a glimpse of Jesus.

Imagine if you and I were as passionate as Zacchaeus about seeking Jesus, our lives would never be the same again. Sometimes all it takes is a determination to keep climbing and to keep moving forward.

NO RISK EQUALS NO REWARD

A story that forever changed my life was one that I read by accident several years ago about a surgeon named Dr. Evan O'Neill Kane.

Dr. Kane believed that some surgeries could be performed without the use of general anesthesia. In his opinion, many simple procedures would be both better and safer without the patient going completely under. What has come to be known as localized or local anesthesia, is a process that blocks the nerves of a specified area in the body that requires surgery. So, in 1921, at the ripe young age of 60, he set out to do the first ever appendectomy under local anesthesia.

FIELD TIP:
"Appendectomy" is a procedure to remove an appendix.

First though, Dr. Kane needed a patient. He began searching for a willing person to help him test this new concept. He talked to friends, put out advertisements and yet none were bold enough to submit to the procedure.

So, Dr. Kane did the **unthinkable**. He operated on himself! Administering the localized anesthetic to his own body, he sat on a gurney, made his incision, and he successfully removed his own appendix.[2]

Oftentimes, when there is something you are passionate about, a yearning deep inside your heart, there is absolutely nothing that will stop you from moving forward. The enemy does not stop working against us because we have a calling, and sometimes he works even harder to stop us. Paul talks in 2 Timothy 1:7 about what can hold us back from our purpose in Christ. Fear!

But I need to encourage you to not let fear paralyze or immobilize you. As Paul said, "For God has not given us a spirit of fear."[3] Instead, God wants us to take risks and live life on the edge. I'm a big believer that God doesn't want us to play it safe with our lives. He is calling us to be risk takers, movers, shakers, change-makers.

Here's the real struggle – we often let fear weigh us down and hold us back from doing something big. I love how John Gardner puts it, "One of the reasons why mature people stop growing and learning is that they become less and less willing to take risks."[4] When was the last time you took a risk? Even a small one, like ordering something new at a restaurant or buying a shirt without trying it on? How can we expect God to trust us with His biggest plans if we do not trust Him with our most mundane choices?

Everyday people shy away from the **unthinkable** because they are afraid that they may fail. Some may avoid accomplishing things for God because they want to save face with others. The truth is that without any risk there can be no great reward. God has created you with a desire to do something big with your life so stop playing it safe. Now is the moment, this is the time to step out in faith and take some risks. We cannot wait until tomorrow comes to begin taking risks for God, because we are not guaranteed tomorrow, so let us start today, right now, at this very moment.

The enemy has a way of making us think that failing is the worst possible outcome. The world wants us to believe that to fail means we are failures, but if we know God's Word, we know that cannot be true. In the end, sitting back in the fear of failure and refusing to step out and attempt what God is calling us to do will leave us with more regret than failure ever will.

In fact, on our team we encourage failure. If you are not failing every once in a while, then you are not engaging in things that are difficult enough. If you and I are not willing to take risks, then odds are we will never accomplish anything **unthinkable** with our lives.

DON'T STOP ON SIX

God never promised us an easy life. Sometimes in our walk with the Lord, we must make tough decisions. For my wife and I, the call to start a brand-new, life-giving church was the beginning of a season of difficult choices. When God called us to plant this church in the heart of Oklahoma City, we were scared to death. This meant uprooting our family from a safe community and a well-loved church. For seven years, we had built a support system of close friends who were like family. We would be saying goodbye to them, as well as, on a more practical note, giving up health insurance and a steady salary. All of this change to move to an unfamiliar city to pursue the dream God placed in our hearts.

This shift in our ministry direction was incredibly exciting, but the unknowns had us on the edge of our seats. After wrestling with what God was speaking to us, along with the right timing to begin the journey, the tension of both stepping out in faith and leaving the comfort of the known was dragging us down. I will never forget a particular phone call from Kate. I was on the way home from a trip to Tulsa, Oklahoma. My phone rang and as I answered I could hear the serious tones in Kate's voice. Her urgency told me that this was a different kind of conversation, and that I needed to really focus on what she had to say. Not just passively listen, but actively hear her. Often the closest thing to an audible voice from the Holy Spirit in my life is my wife. She's such an incredible life partner.

On this particular day, she decided to call after listening to a sermon. She had just been listening to a message by Pastor Steven Furtick about the Israelites marching around the walls of Jericho.[5] In the message, Pastor Steven throws out this question. "What would have happened if the Israelites had quit marching around the city after the sixth time?"

You may not know the story, so let me recap it quickly for you. God spoke to the leader of the Israelites, Joshua, and told him to rally the people of Israel. He commanded them to march around the great city one time for six days, and seven times on the seventh day.[6]

If we look back to Genesis 12, God told the children of Israel that they would one day inhabit the Promised Land. At this point in our story, the Israelites had been wandering in the wilderness for 40 years, waiting to see God's Word fulfilled. All of Israel had crossed the Jordan River, a natural border between the promised land and the wilderness.

Joshua led God's people to the outer walls of Jericho. It was there that God gave instructions on how to march. Now, Jericho was a heavily armed and guarded city. Historians tell us the walls surrounding it were so thick chariots could have been driven on the top of them. That is massive!

So, the people of Israel, all two million of them, began to march. Silently. Like it was a funeral procession. Just walking. Imagine the people from Jericho watching from the wall, it must have been an eerie sight. The Israelites did not fight, they did not talk, they simply walked, and looked foolish doing so.

So, let's get back to the question my wife called me to discuss. What would have happened if the Israelites had quit marching around the city after the sixth time? What would have happened if they had begun to march around the city, and completed their rounds through the sixth day but failed to continue all the way through on day seven? We do not know, but I doubt it would have made it into the Bible as a lesson on walking in faith. Based on other times where God's chosen people missed the mark, I have a suspicion that nothing would have happened. At the very least nothing good. God asked for their faith and obedience, even in the face of criticism.

Why did God ask this of them? For the same reason Naaman had to dip seven times in the Jordan.[8] It's the same reason that Jesus asked the servants at the wedding in Cana to fill the stone jars to the brim with water.[9] God told the Israelites to do it, and in order to see their miracle, they needed to march around the wall – not five or six times, but seven.

During that phone conversation, my wife revealed what she had learned from God, "It's time to step out in faith and move our family. We can't keep waiting, we can't stop on six. We have to step out in faith." We knew our lives would be forever changed, but that day we decided to let our leadership know our plans. We listed our home and it sold only two weeks later by owner. A month later we had a double closing on both the home we sold and the new home that we were purchasing in Oklahoma City. When God says go, He makes the way possible.

We moved our family on June 16th, 2014 and began building the team to start the church. With just eight people in our living room, dreaming about the church that God was calling us to become, we had taken the first step into the unknown, into the **unthinkable**. We were underdogs with a dream, but God had a different plan – a plan that would change our name forever.

THEY CALL ME TIGER

One Sunday a young pastor was invited over to the home of a family in his church. He was single, new to ministry and new to the church. Little did he know what he was getting himself into that Sunday afternoon.

As the man unfastened his seatbelt and made his way to the front door, noises could be heard as he reached out to ring the doorbell. He tensed up being unaccustomed to the sounds coming from the other side of the door.

The husband welcomed the pastor in, introduced his wife, and urged him to have a seat on the couch. Stepping over toys, puzzle pieces, and crayons littering the floor, the pastor nestled into a spot on the couch that was mostly free of clutter.

As the three of them tried to get acquainted, the noise persisted. The source was a rambunctious three-year old girl. She carried on causing interruptions by running, yelling, screaming, and shouting. Her mother apologized saying, "We're so sorry that it's hard to talk. That's our daughter, we call her Tiger."

The couple moved to dinner and still the same challenges ensued. There was barely a quiet moment as Tiger persisted. She demanded attention by interrupting the conversation, throwing food, and dropping her bottle on purpose.

Eventually the meal finished and the pastor left. However, several months later, he once again received an invitation to the same family's home for dinner. As their pastor, he gave a hesitant yes not wanting to disappoint them, but the events of their last get-together were seared into his memory. Reluctantly, he went.

As he pulled into the driveway he had already begun to sweat profusely. The memories of his last dinner were coming back vividly. He closed the car door and headed towards the front steps of their home, bracing himself for the worst. Surprisingly, as he approached the door, he did not hear a thing.

He rang the doorbell and once again the husband of the home opened the door. "Come on in Pastor," he said. The pastor was absolutely floored. The front room of the house was clean, but that wasn't what shocked him the most. As he scanned the room, he noticed their little daughter, Tiger, sitting in the corner at a small desk with a coloring book and a sweet smile on her face. He was again invited to sit down.

Still not convinced, he waited for the moment when Tiger would show her true colors. However, she continued to play quietly, and sat by herself coloring contently.

It came time for dinner and the meal was wonderful. The conversation was uninterrupted and quite pleasant. The pastor's curiosity could not be silenced any longer. He mustered up the courage to ask, "What has happened to Tiger? She has behaved herself so well this afternoon. What did you guys do?"

The father smiled, nodded and replied, "Well Pastor, we made a major discovery. For the first few years of her life, we called her Tiger and that's what she acted like. We realized that we needed to call her by a new nickname. So, we started calling her 'Princess' and this is how she has acted ever since."

A NEW NAME

I believe that one of the greatest areas of struggle in our lives lies in determining our identity and knowing ourselves fully.

Matthew Keller has written an incredible book, *God of the Underdogs*, that I would recommend you read. In it he describes many excuses that keep us from living out our true God-given destiny. He submits that most of the time our mistake happens when we allow others to name us, thus rooting our identity in what they say about us. We may look like underdogs, but God wants to give us a new name.

In Matthew 16:17-18, Jesus is talking to his disciple, Simon Peter. The name "Simon" when translated from the original Greek means *"reed"* or *"one who sways"*.[10] Picture a person who has planted their feet in the sand at the beach. They step down and their feet sink and squish. Sand is not the best foundation for a steady footing.

That was Simon, or at least what he was named. In turn, it was who he had become. When Simon's parents named him, whether they intended to or not, they were calling him wishy-washy, a person who swayed back and forth, and he began to live that out. Sometimes when people are called something for so long, they internalize it, and it becomes a self-fulfilling prophecy.

However, verse 18 tells us that Jesus had some other plans for Simon's life. The passage says, "But I tell you that you are Peter."[11] The name "Peter" translates to "petros" or "the rock".[12] In other words, Jesus was telling Peter that what his parents said did not matter. He was getting a new name, no longer swaying in his faith, but remaining steadfast. Like a rock. He even goes so far as to say that the church would be built upon him. Simon, now called Peter, would become someone that God could depend on, and he would go on to do the *unthinkable* for the kingdom of God.

The Bible tells us that on the day of Pentecost, just 50 days after the resurrection of Jesus, Peter was among 120 people who were in the upper room praying when the Holy Spirit came upon them with power.[13] Acts 2 then recounts that he stood up, preached the gospel and more than 3,000 people became followers of Jesus that day. Jesus gave him a new name, and it changed everything.

God has given you a new name as well. As 1 John 3 says, today you are no longer slaves in your sin. God has paid an ultimate price for you. You and I belong to Him, and He has given us a new identity. Today we are called the children of God and because of that He is going to empower you to do the *unthinkable*.

On April 5th, 2015, we launched our church. It was one of the hardest things that we have ever done and yet, also the most rewarding. Since that day God has continued to change lives. We have seen that change fuel people to find their purpose. In all of my best imaginations, my deepest desires, and my grandest dreams, I could not have envisioned the life I am leading or the opportunities that God has given me.

In the coming chapters, we will look at more miracles that came from *unthinkable* choices and dig deeper into how we can position ourselves to stand up to our fears in those pivotal seasons. Let us take a moment and be thankful for a couple lessons I learned, and ones I want to encourage you with.

I am thankful that God did not let us stop on six. I am thankful that even when things were stacked against us, we chose to climb. Most of all, I am thankful that God continues to urge us to draw near to Him and to pursue *His* plan for our lives.

The same God that looked at an orphan girl named Esther, and saw a queen, gave me a new name. The God that sought out a shepherd boy named David and called him a mighty warrior, looks at us underdogs. He sees us for who we really are, His children, who are called to His purpose and are able to accomplish the ***unthinkable*** for Him!

FIELD NOTES

KEY IDEAS:

- Don't stop on six. Don't give up! You never know just how close you are to the promise of God for your life.
- Do not let other people define you. God knows your name and who you truly are.
- One reason people stop growing is because they become less and less willing to take big risks.

FOLLOW-UP QUESTIONS:

1. Remember a time in your life when you felt like an underdog? Did you still win? If so, what did you do to beat the odds?
2. Is there a season you are walking in right now that makes you want to give up before you cross the finish line?
3. Like Simon Peter, has anything been spoken over you that negatively defined who you are? How can you break the hold those words have over your life?

FIELD NOTES

CHAPTER THREE · CHAPTER THREE · CHAPTER THREE · CHAPTER THREE · CHAPTER THREE · CHAPTER THREE ·

GETTING TO THE SPOT

5When Jesus reached the spot, he looked up and said to him, "Zacchaeus, come down immediately. I must stay at your house today." 6So he came down at once and welcomed him gladly.

Luke 19:5-6

When I was a kid watching television, the technology that we have today did not exist. There I go sounding like an old man, but unfortunately, it is true. I am a football fan. I love to watch college football games. I used to live in Oklahoma (I'll explain this further in the last chapter) and in Oklahoma, college football is all the rage. When I lived there, I enjoyed going to games with my good friend, because he had season tickets to Sooners games.

However, one advantage that we have today as we watch the games on television is called the yards-to-gain line. If you have ever caught a game on television, it is the yellow line that stretches across the screen and that indicates where the ball must cross for the offense to pick up a first down.

If you watch long enough, at some point you will hear the commentator say, "If only they can get inside of the line, they will be able to pick up a first down. If only they can make it to the spot."

ZAC'S SPOT

When we read the Bible, we often fail to grasp the calculated plan Zacchaeus had in Luke 19. It was not rocket science, but he did have a goal in mind. Remember, Zacchaeus was a tax collector. Not a job given to someone lacking in smarts. It was a serious role given out by the government to collect taxes from the people in the community. With that in mind, we are correct to believe that Zac was a very intelligent man. So, when he went up the tree, he must have had a plan – climb the tree, create a scene, and once Jesus arrived at the spot, His attention would fall on Zacchaeus – and the plan worked!

If there is anything that we can learn from Zacchaeus and his ingenuity, it is this – when we position ourselves in the view of Jesus, He will stop and take notice of us. What does this mean for you and me? Quite simply, in a world of people begging for attention, we should seek to be noticed by the right person – Jesus.

If I can borrow from the analogy, there is a time and a tree with your name on it. Daily, Jesus walks by and wants to look up and notice you, but are you putting yourself in the spot where you need to be? Are you making choices that put you in the Lord's path? The joy and fulfillment that come when we are in the middle of God's will are unparalleled but living in God's will does not just happen. If we want to do the *unthinkable* as the devoted follower of Christ that God desires us to be, then we must be intentional in our daily lives and make it happen.

CONVERSATIONS WITH GOD

If we want to live a life that is **unthinkable**, then it is important that we spend time daily in prayer. Paul said in 1 Timothy 2:8, "I want the men everywhere to pray."[1] As humans, we have strong emotions, deep desires, complex internal thoughts and sometimes, these cause us to over complicate prayer. That's right, our own humanity gets in the way. Prayer is not about impressing listening ears, or even impressing God. Prayer in its purest form is a *conversation with God*.

I will never forget visiting a church on the Island of Zanzibar, once pastored by missionary Dr. David Livingstone. Today it serves as a museum to commemorate the end of the slave trade that was once prevalent on the island. Where Livingstone's pulpit now stands there was once a whipping post. In front of large crowds, the slaves were both beaten, then auctioned and sold to the highest bidder.

Livingstone's actions helped to end slavery on the island and what was once a place of hopelessness and devastation transformed into a place of hope and life in Christ. This man, who was once a stranger, quickly became like family to the African people.

Along with his work to end slavery, Livingstone was known for being a man of prayer. A story from his days on the mission field tells of a time when he became extremely sick. He was older in age and his health was failing fast. Being too weak to sit up on his own, he called for assistance so that he might kneel and pray. The attendant assisted him and quietly slipped out of the tent allowing Livingstone unimpeded time with the Lord. Time passed, 30 minutes, then an hour, with the attendant knowing that at some point he would have to help him back off his knees and back onto his cot. However, Livingstone had not finished praying. An hour and a half, then two hours, and still he was not ready. Finally, after three hours, the servant slipped in to check on Livingstone and return him to his cot to rest. It was then that he discovered that the missionary had died while on his knees in prayer. He had passed into eternity, while having a conversation with God.[2]

My point in sharing this amazing story is to remind us that so often we over complicate prayer. We make it more difficult than it needs to be. Prayer is spending time talking to God. Livingstone knew how and every time I think about that story, I cannot help but think about how he went from talking to God by faith in one moment to seeing Him face-to-face the next. How incredible is that? Prayer and building a connection with God is so very important.

We must not forget that Jesus set an extremely high importance on prayer. So integral was prayer in his daily life that in Mark 1:35 it says, "Early in the morning, while it was still dark Jesus got up and went off to a solitary place to pray." Just as Jesus took time in the morning to pray, so should we. As 1 Timothy 2:8 says it's what God desires most from us (my paraphrase). All he wants is to spend time each day with us!

In his book, *The Dare*, Josh Mayo suggests walking out, "The 10/10 Plan".[3] The 10/10 Plan is simply spending ten minutes both reading the Bible and ten minutes in prayer each day. For those who struggle with spending large amounts of time in prayer, The 10/10 plan is a great place to start.

Just like anything you do, progressing towards a deeper relationship with God takes effort, and forming meaningful habits is the best way to create space for growth in your

Christian walk. Prayer and spending time in God's Word will only become a pillar in your life if you make them a habit. The old adage rings true here that practice makes perfect, and in this case, practice makes permanent. The bottom line is that God just wants to spend time with us. If we want to live out the **unthinkable**, then prayer needs to become an essential part of our daily routine.

THE ACCLAMATION PROCESS

Three days into the hike to Uhuru Peak on Kilimanjaro there was a moment that was deeply concerning. As a climber, the greatest fear after having traveled a great distance is to be halfway up the mountain and be forced to turn around to go home. In fact, my climbing partner, Nathan and I were so concerned that we went to a doctor and had been prescribed medication to help us with our oxygen intake. The *ace* as we called it, would help us to breathe easier while at a higher altitude, but sometimes it does not matter – some people just cannot acclimate to the change in oxygen levels.

Much like Jesus, acclimation is not a respecter of persons. Often, overweight grandfathers have finished the climb while marathon runners have failed. All that matters is what each individual's body will allow them to do.

Next is an excerpt from my climbing journal that paints a picture of what transpired with Nathan and I, on day three...

KILIMANJARO, BARRONCO CAMP
WEDNESDAY, SEPTEMBER 18TH, 2013

We woke up knowing that this was a huge day for us. It was acclamation day. As we left Shira Camp and headed for Lava Tower, we would be climbing up to 14,950 feet before heading to Barranco Camp and an altitude of 12,000 feet. It would be a good test to see if our bodies were up for the challenge.

Leaving Shira Camp, we began a gradual steep climb. It took us through the moorlands. There were pretty flowers and large boulders there. At one point the climb became significantly steep and challenging. As we were inching one step at a time (pole-pole as they say in Swahili) it was apparent that Nate wasn't doing well. What we later found out was that Nate's oxygen level was great, but he could not start his morning hike on a big breakfast.

Oh, by the way - did I mention I had a major problem last night? I went to the toilet, running three different times. I found out that the fruit mango really means "man go" if you eat too much of it.

So, we made it to Lava Tower, a stunning rock formation. We also got a glimpse of the glaciers on Uhuru for the first time up close and personal. Wow!

We then headed to Barronco camp. It was quite a bit down-hill, and the palm trees and waterfalls were awesome to take in. We settled in camp. That night at dinner, Rodin had a proposal for us. Tomorrow was going to be a short 2½ hour trip to Karanga with another short trip the following day to Barafu Camp, otherwise known as "Base Camp". His proposal was to do Karanga and Barafu in just one day. The trip would be about six hours long.

Rodin noticed that Nate wasn't doing well in the mornings and that I struggled in the cold. So, he pitched climbing the summit in the early morning rather than at mid-night as is traditionally done. It would shorten our trip from 7 days to 6. We decided to head for Karanga, eat a hot lunch and evaluate from there.

Acclimating is a big deal and on day three, we were faced with a sobering reality that I might have to make the climb without Nathan. While I did not want to continue up the mountain without my friend, the need to acclimate will always win out. Thankfully, after taking it slow for a while, he was able to press on.

All of that to say, having a healthy prayer life takes time to develop. It takes some time to acclimate. The feeling of discomfort that goes hand-in-hand with acclimation can make you discouraged, but do not let it get you down. Change is hard for everyone, not just mountain climbers. The key is to take it one step at a time and be consistent.

One of my favorite quotes is from Smith Wigglesworth. He said, "I don't often spend more than half an hour in prayer at one time, but I never go more than half an hour without praying."[4]

We must discipline ourselves daily and sometimes we must force our way to the place where we can encounter Jesus. We must strive to meet Him at the spot. It is through the work of creating a healthy habit of prayer in our lives that we can grow and acclimate to the higher heights God has for us.

THE CIRCLE MAKER

One of my favorite books was written by my friend, Mark Batterson. It's called *The Circle Maker*. In the book, Mark details the saga of Honi, the Circle Maker, a man who lived in the 400-year period between the Old and New Testament, a man who was determined to see God answer his prayers.[5]

Honi knew how to pray, often his reputation preceded him. It was not uncommon for people to pass by his home and hear him praying. The story begins at a time when the city where Honi lived was experiencing a severe drought. It had been years since the last time people had seen rain and they were desperate. They went to Honi's home and began knocking. He was their last resort, their only hope. When he came to answer the door, the city leaders began begging and pleading for him to come out and to pray for a breakthrough.

Honi acquiesced, moving to the center of the city in dramatic fashion, staff in hand, he turned three hundred and sixty degrees as he drew a circle in the sand. He then stepped into the circle, and began to cry out to God saying, "I will not move from this circle until God hears my prayer, now Lord, send your rain."

Honi prayed with tenacity, with determination and called out to God fervently until the first drop of rain fell to the ground. One by one the drops fell, a fine mist into a steady shower, then an all-out downpour. As the rain fell from the sky, people crowded the streets and danced for joy. Children played in the rain. Several had never even seen it rain before.

All of this happened because one man drew a circle, began to pray, and refused to give up until God answered. I want to echo the words of my friend Mark and encourage you to be a circle maker, to pray bold prayers and keep the faith even when years of drought have set in. Do not give up because God will answer our prayers, but He answers them in his own timing.

I am a circle maker. I have drawn circles in my prayer journal, I have even walked circles around buildings and city blocks. There is power in simple patterns and the more we circle, the more we acclimate ourselves to an attitude of prayer. When we pray, we are practicing getting to the spot where we can see Jesus and He can see us.

In 2014, my friend Mike Santiago planted Focus Church, in the city of Apex, North Carolina, just outside of Raleigh. Years later, the church experienced some challenging times. It was mid-June when their location, a school they rented from, declined to renew their lease, and gave them two weeks to move out. You read that right, Mike only had two weeks to find a new place for his growing congregation to meet. He did the only thing he could think of, he prayed. He also worked like it all depended on him, but he prayed like it all depended on God.

Within that time frame, the church secured a new meeting place, a local country club. But after only two weeks, the director informed Mike that Focus Church was causing too much wear and tear on the club. There were just too many attendees coming each week. They also gave Mike two weeks to find yet another meeting place. Later, Focus began meeting on Saturdays in a church belonging to another congregation. While all this was happening, behind the scenes, God was working.

Rewind back to the unfortunate day in June when Mike was first contacted by the school. It just so happened that 30 minutes away, a struggling church was saying goodbye to their pastor. One church was looking for a shepherd to lead them, and another was looking for a home. In August that same summer, that shepherdless church voted unanimously to become Focus Church, and a healthy, thriving church family was formed. That same church now meets in a 77,000 square foot facility on 66 acres. They have multiple campuses and are doing amazing things for the Kingdom throughout North Carolina. All of this happened because Mike chose to put his focus on God. He chose to draw his circle in the sand and refused to move until God showed up.

When we as Christians put the amount of focus on prayer that Honi or Mike did, it shows God where our hearts are. When we have our hearts aligned with God, and we put our trust in Him, it is awesome to see what happens.

EMPTY CIRCLES

I have made it a practice over the last decade to circle things in prayer. As I have mentioned before, I've literally drawn circles in my notebook around things that I am focusing on and bringing before God. I've literally gone on prayer walks in specific locations. Praying circles is about intentionally taking things to God in prayer.

However, just because I work on being a circle maker doesn't mean everything, I have circled ends up the way I anticipated. In fact, after spending some significant time in prayer, there have been moments that I realized I was circling the wrong things.

Through those times, God has assured me it is better to circle the wrong thing, to spend time praying about what I think is His will, but miss the mark, than to never circle anything in prayer at all. I have found that God opens doors for us through that process of circling that would never open otherwise. Sometimes I have found myself thanking God for those empty circles.

In September of 2016, I began circling an old run-down church building on the corner of 30th and Hudson. This location was brought to our attention as a potential permanent home for the church we had planted in Oklahoma City. We then attempted to contact the owner to negotiate terms to purchase the building.

I began to circle that particular building in prayer on Wednesdays. As we waited to hear back, I would put in my ear buds, turn on worship music and literally circle the block in the Paseo District of Oklahoma City where the building was located. This continued until March of the following year. For more than six months, I circled that building. In the rain, snow, as seasons changed, I circled and still nothing. All the while, unbeknownst to me, God was at work.

Late on a Thursday night near the end of March, I was having dinner in Washington, D.C. while at a church launch event, when I received a phone call. It was a friend that attended our church and was a commercial real estate broker. He called to say that at a dinner with some associates in Oklahoma City, he had heard about an opportunity to purchase a building. He had told his colleagues of our never-ending search to find the right location for our church family. One of the brokers at the table said, "I think I may have something."

That following Monday, we arrived at the dilapidated brick building that had sat vacant for the past 17 years. Formerly a warehouse, it had changed hands several times and though the stench of an unused building filled our nostrils, and the patina of time clouded our eyes, the expansive space spoke to us. We could see the potential. The building had *good bones*, like you might imagine hearing on a fixer upper television show and it had an intriguing backstory. Formerly the space housed a venue called Bricktown Joker's Comedy Club, which in its heyday had played host to several aspiring comedians like Chris Rock, Carrot Top, and Jay Leno. Sadly, with the rise in popularity of situational comedies on mainstream television, Bricktown Joker's closed their doors on December 31st, 1999, and there it sat, empty, awaiting its reinvention, until April of 2017.

Through a series of miracles, we purchased the building and began renovations. Today The Bridge in Bricktown is a non-profit with weekly worship services, office space, and serves as an event center. It is also the home of Landing Coffee Company, a coffee shop, open seven days a week in downtown Oklahoma City.

Sometimes we circle the wrong things in prayer. We focus on what we want and what we think God intends for us, but we only see in part. He knows the whole. I tend to believe that God views our errant focus, our empty circles and He honors that. We might have empty circles, but in return God leads us to His circles, filled with miracles we never could have dreamt of.

SPEAK LORD, YOUR SERVANT IS LISTENING

Now, talking to God is only part of the conversation. I am a big believer that we also need to learn how to listen for the voice of God. While waiting on the voice of God can feel weird, and to the world might look foolish, it is one of the biggest things we as Christ followers can do to move deeper into relationship with Him.

A wonderful part of getting into the Word of God is that you can be encouraged by the people who follow God in ancient times, and you can learn from the encounters they had. One such person was Samuel, and in 1 Samuel 3, we find his story. But before we can fully grasp the weight of this, we need to investigate who Samuel was and learn his origin story in 1 Samuel 1.

It all began with a woman named Hannah, who was desperate to have a child. As the narrative opens, we find her inconsolable in her need, and pacing the temple, circling her infertility in prayer.

The Bible declares her prayers so fervent, so intense, that her lips were noticeably moving as she prayed silently, under her breath. So passionate were her pleas that she caught the attention of the temple priest, Eli.

As Eli approached young Hannah, he began to scold her for coming into the house of God while intoxicated. Hannah swiftly explained herself, she was not drunk, but was earnestly pleading with God that He might bless her with a son. She went on to proclaim that if God opened her womb and allowed her to bear a son, she would bring him to the temple and dedicate him to the Lord – giving Him her son into a life of service to God and to the work of the ministry. God saw her circle in prayer, He heard her plea, and she became pregnant. She bore a son and named him Samuel.

We can now skip forward to chapter three, to a time in Israel's history when the voice of God was rarely heard and also a pivotal moment in the life of young eight-year-old Samuel. In the early hours of the morning, as Eli the priest and Samuel lay asleep, Samuel hears a voice call out his name in the darkness. Thinking it is his master Eli, he promptly arises, enters the chamber where Eli resides and says, "Here I am, you called me." Imagine Eli, awoken from a deep sleep, and most likely annoyed or perhaps worried replying, "I did not call; go back and lie down."

So, after returning to bed, Samuel once again heard the voice in the darkness call to him, and again he went to Eli who promptly sent him back to sleep.

If you have ever cared for young children, put yourself in Eli's place, a young child in your care, hearing his name called in the night, most of us would have dismissed this as a dream, a sleepy delirium, but not Eli. When Samuel heard the voice call a third time, and again came to his master's chambers, Eli realized that it was the Lord God calling to the boy. So, Eli told Samuel, "Go and lie down, and if he calls you, say, 'Speak Lord, for your servant is listening.'"[6]

This scripture is such a potent reminder that hearing God's voice takes practice. God has never spoken to me audibly–probably because if He ever did, He knows the experience would scare me to death. Nevertheless, there were seasons and instances in my life when I felt God speaking into my heart about something. There is nothing like the sense of peace you feel when God places His dreams within you.

That sense of peace came the very moment I first saw my wife. I knew that I was going to marry her, I was so confident that when I returned to my dorm, I told my friends and began to journal about it. I still have that journal today, and it encourages me to remember that before I even had my first conversation with Kate, I was already praying for her by name. Some would call that being a stalker! I choose to believe that God was just giving me hope and assurance that I wasn't going to be single for the rest of my life.

100 HOURS OF PRAYER

Another key moment when I felt strongly that God was speaking to me was in December of 2014. During this time, we were building our team and holding meetings in preparation to plant our campus in Oklahoma City. This burden from God came to me during a night of prayer and communion. I felt God tell me to commit to spending 100 hours in prayer between New Year's Day and Easter Sunday. With Easter falling on April 5th of the coming year, it would only give me 95 days to make that happen.

Now, I need you to know something about me. I believe in the power of prayer. I believe in the importance of prayer. However, it's every bit of the word "*discipline*" to me. It's tough and often I find it both painful and stretching. I know some people who wake up early in the morning and naturally fall on their faces in prayer. It comes easy for them. I'm not one of those people.

Praying 100 hours of prayer was a definite spiritual challenge. I felt that God was specifically asking that it be 100 hours of sacrificial time, not simply praying while I was in the office, but on my personal time. God was calling me to give up hours of my mornings, my lunches, or my evenings to pray.

> **I DON'T OFTEN SPEND MORE THAN HALF AN HOUR IN PRAYER AT ONE TIME, BUT I NEVER GO MORE THAN HALF AN HOUR WITHOUT PRAYING.**[4]

Now, during this season, we were in the process of searching for a launch location for our church plant. For almost 15 months, we had been looking, but to no avail. Yet, despite our growing weariness, God had a plan.

As I began to pray, fast, and seek God, we were led to a building. On January 15th, we found The Will Rogers Theater, a space that was completely off our radar. We then began to purchase equipment while we prepared our team. After pre-launch services in March, we commenced regular services in April. What day in April? The 5th, Easter Sunday – exactly 100 hours of prayer later.

MISSED OPPORTUNITIES

Thinking over the life of my Christian walk, I can reflect on the many opportunities God has placed in my path. I wish I could look back and say that in every instance I took God's plan over my own. That I allowed the subtle nudging of the Holy Spirit in my life to guide my daily steps, but I have missed so many of God's open doors. I have probably missed hundreds more than I have answered. So, in looking at your own walk, do not get discouraged, God knows we are imperfect, and He can still use us in our weakness.

I will never forget the day I walked into the grocery store after work to pick up a two-liter of Coke Zero. As I made my way to the drink aisle, I saw the Coke guy stocking the shelves. I wanted to be polite, so I asked him how he was doing. His reply caught me off guard as he said, "I'm living the dream, man." No disrespect, but I never met anyone who grew up dreaming of restocking Coca-Cola products for a living. I have heard of kids wanting to be a doctor, a lawyer, and a firefighter, but never the Coke distributor. Trust me, there are days in my ministry when I do not feel like I am living the dream either. So, in that moment, reaching for my two-liter, I was caught off-guard by his response.

As I stood there in the soda aisle, I felt the Holy Spirit prodding me, *"Ask him why he's living his dream."*

I froze.

The Holy Spirit continued, *"If he doesn't answer, 'Because I have a relationship with Jesus,' then you can tell him about me and why you are living your dream."*

The thoughts lingered, circled, but I shook it off. I was only there to grab a bottle of pop so I could go home and unwind. After all, it had been a long day of ministry. I sought to justify ignoring the whole ordeal, and in doing so I walked away. To this day, I wonder what could have happened in that moment. I continue to pray that God would help me be obedient and to not miss any more opportunities to respond when He speaks. Much like this next story I want to share with you.

A few years ago, the Stevens family who attended our church plant in Oklahoma City were shopping at Forever 21. While there, they met a little girl who had lost her hair from treatment she had just completed at a nearby hospital. God spoke to their hearts to pray for her and her family. As they introduced themselves to the family, they discovered that this little girl and her parents were from England and that they had traveled all the way to the US for some specialized treatment. They were now on their journey back home.

When the Stevens asked to pray for them, right there in the store, the parents broke down into tears. After prayer they said, "Our flight to England was delayed an entire day, and now we know why. You have given us hope and we know that God is going to take care of us and our daughter."

When we listen to the voice of God, and act out of obedience, God uses us to do the **unthinkable**. While we might not always have experiences like the Stevens family, God uses our willingness to help grow others' faith in Him. To encourage, to comfort, and even to grow our own faith.

We are so limited in our view of the world. There is no way the Stevens could have known the impact that a short conversation would have on a family from England, but God knew. He gives us all opportunities just like this one to show His love to humanity every single day.

BLIND OBEDIENCE

There are innumerable, **unthinkable** God-appointments that get me excited as a pastor. In all of my years in ministry, there have been so many beautiful flashes of God within the ordinary moments of life. They are often spurred on by seasons of blind obedience. Seasons where God moves in a situation, rocks our lives, and boosts our faith.

Several years ago, I spoke to our church family about obeying the voice of God. I shared about my missed opportunity at the grocery store, encouraging our church family to listen for the voice of God and to trust Him.

That Sunday, during the altar time, a young man, Josh, felt led to pray for a first-time guest that morning. Josh initially felt fearful that he was off base and so he brushed it off. However, the Holy Spirit continued to prompt him as the service concluded. As the final prayer ended and the people were congregating, Josh, unable to ignore that still small voice any longer, took off after Brian into the parking lot. He hastily caught up with him and introduced himself. Then, coming up for breath Josh said, "I feel like I'm just supposed to pray with you. Is that ok? Is there anything I can pray with you about?"

Brian broke down and said, "Yes," and he confided about his struggle with an alcohol addiction. That day, as they stood together praying in the church parking lot, Brian experienced the **unthinkable**, an act of love, initiated by God and carried out through Josh. Brian left knowing God loved him, knowing he was not meant to struggle through his addiction alone. Josh's act of obedience was not the reason Brian felt that way, that was completely God, but it would not have happened at that appointed time if Josh had not stepped out in faith.

WAKE UP CALL

Climbing Kilimanjaro was a personal dream for a considerable amount of time. The main setback preventing my expedition was the expense of such a trip. The trek up Kilimanjaro is by no means a budget friendly venture, especially on a penny-pinching youth pastor's salary. So, like any reasonable person, I kept my dream bottled up, only sharing it with my wife and a few close friends – also pastors with equally tight budgets who share my pain. Late one August evening in 2012, as the heat of the night pressed in, I lay in bed, tossing and turning. In my bedroom in northwest Oklahoma, God began to re-ignite a dream inside of me, one that I had not thought about in over two years. In the past, the dream felt like it was far off and unattainable, but this time was different. This time God gave me peace in my heart, dropped some ideas in my mind, and said, "Go for it!" One thing I have learned is that we can depend on God to wake us up from our sleep, to shake up our lives, even in the middle of the night, and when we find ourselves unexpectedly woken, or unable to sleep, we should take a moment and ask God what He is wanting to tell us. We should respond to His call just like Samuel did.

After my own sleepless night, the next few days were filled with phone calls, looking into the logistics and figuring out the financing. Soon, everything had fallen into place in a way that only God could orchestrate.

The longer you walk with God, the more you will learn to recognize the perfect peace in the wake of His movements. Not quite audible, the prodding of the Spirit of God at work can almost be missed but it is always right, and always on time. As you already know, God saw the dream in my heart, and paved the way for it to become a reality.

So that week, I made those important phone calls, and not only did I talk to the right people, but it was the right timing. Doesn't that sound just like God? Always right, and always on time, and the rest of the story only gets better! The financing came through and we did it!

When you couple a discerning spirit with big faith, God-dreams happen!

OPEN MY EYES

One of my favorite stories in scripture is the story of Elisha and his servant who were both on the run fleeing from the King of Aram in 2 Kings 6. Up to this point, the Lord had protected

Elisha and his servant, misleading would-be attackers and guiding the men to places of safety. The men would hear from God and move away from harm. This happened so often, that the king demanded his officials root out the mole who was tipping Elisha off ahead of time. How cool is that?

On one particular night, the king's army finally surrounded the camp of Elisha. As his servant peaked out the tent that next morning, he stood there terrified, as he surveyed the massive army surrounding them. Scripture doesn't tell us this, but I think he might have even wet his pants. He cried out in fear, "Lord save us!"

Elisha, on the other hand, looked out of the tent and he was able to see a much different scenario. Elisha was able to see something that the servant could not see. Using the gift of discernment from the Holy Spirit, Elisha's gaze swept beyond the army of Aram and fixed upon the army of the Lord that was ready to protect them.[7]

Having discernment is the ability to hear God's voice and see through the lens of His spiritual eyes. See things that are not common to people looking and listening in the physical. Discernment is a gift that God has for us. The catch is that we must be willing to act upon it. As we move past our preconceived notions about how God might speak to us, we can practice discernment in our lives and grow in our giftings as we mature in our relationship with God. If we don't use it, we could lose it. If we do activate the gift of discernment and use it, then our gift will grow and mature and God promises to do the **unthinkable** through us!

Do you believe God is willing and able to do something incredible through you? I know I do because I've experienced it! You can too. As you move into God's path and position yourself to grow deeper in your relationship with him, I challenge you to put two components into practice. You should strive to pray and then listen. These two things will prepare you to get to the spot, and like he did to Zacchaeus, Jesus will see you and He will say, "Hey friend, come down. I'm going to come over to your house today."

FIELD NOTES

KEY IDEAS:

- When we put ourselves in the pathway of Jesus, He will stop and take notice of us.
- It is better to circle the wrong thing in prayer than it is to never circle anything at all.
- When you couple discernment with big faith God-dreams are fulfilled.

FOLLOW-UP QUESTIONS:

1. When is the best time for you to meet with God on a daily basis?
3. Do you have a set time with God?
5. Have you ever heard God speak to you? What did He say?
7. Who in your life could be an Eli for you? Is there someone who could act as a sounding board, that could help you learn to hear God's voice?

FIELD
NOTES

PART TWO

IT WAS HIS UNTHINKABLE LOVE THAT MOVED HIM TO STEP IN FOR US.

IT WAS HIS UNTHINKABLE LOVE THAT MOVED HIM TO STEP IN FOR US.

IT WAS HIS UNTHINKABLE LOVE THAT MOVED HIM TO STEP IN FOR US.

IT WAS HIS UNTHINKABLE LOVE THAT MOVED HIM TO STEP IN FOR US.

We spent the first three chapters talking about what the *unthinkable* looks like in the lives of Christ followers. You heard about climbing trees and mountains, running marathons, and walking circles. You may be thinking, "No way, not me, too outrageous".

I can understand that, but often, the things followers of Jesus do, appear to be *unthinkable* to the people around them. It is God's desire that, as a follower of Christ, you and I attempt to live, walking through these same *unthinkable* things every day with our lives.

You don't have to ride a bicycle for days on end or jump out of a plane to find yourself in God's *unthinkable* moments. The next section of the book will give you practical examples for how to cultivate your life with intention, walking into the *unthinkable* each day while pointing others to Jesus.

ARE YOU READY? LET'S GO!

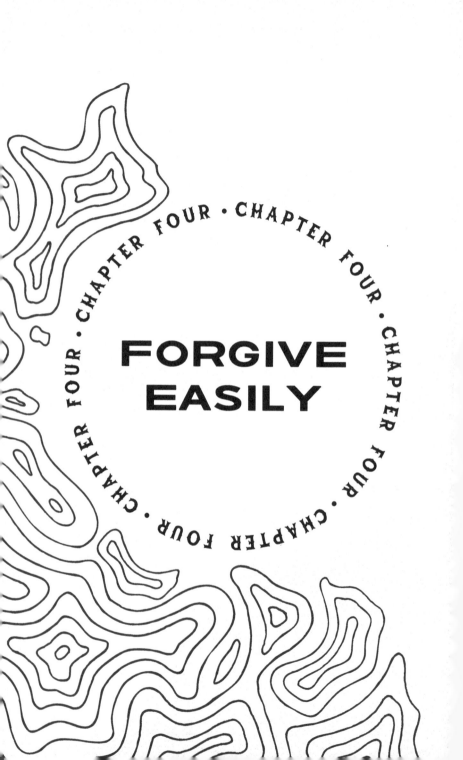

CHAPTER FOUR · CHAPTER FOUR · CHAPTER FOUR · CHAPTER FOUR · CHAPTER FOUR · CHAPTER FOUR

FORGIVE EASILY

[8]Zacchaeus just stood there, a little stunned. He stammered apologetically, "Master, I give away half my income to the poor—and if I'm caught cheating, I pay four times the damages."

Luke 19:8 MSG

know that forgiveness is a tough subject for many people, but I believe that the life of one who walks in the **unthinkable**, is marked by the ability to forgive easily. We must strive for this godly forgiveness in our lives because our ability to recognize what His forgiveness looks like informs our Christian walk, more, perhaps, than anything else. God's forgiveness is at the center of everything, and we should take time to ponder that.

Ephesians 4:32 tells us to forgive others, "just as in Christ God forgave us."[1] And what we have to realize is that according to this passage, forgiveness is not really a suggestion it's an instruction that we are given by God to follow.

DEATH BEFORE LIFE

When I was a young person and in my late teens, I came home one Christmas to some discouraging news. I was a very cynical Bible College student. It was my junior year and by this point I had become really good at judging right and wrong and holding up standards for other people – which by the way is NOT a good thing!

It was on a night in December that my oldest brother Jeff called me to the steps of our stairway at my house, and he began to tell me about his new life choices. I listened intently, as an air of dread overcame me, and I found myself unable to support his decisions. Suffice to say, I made myself exceptionally clear! Now, in hindsight, my response was not Christ-like, and it placed a strain on our relationship for more than a decade.

Fast-forward to the fall of 2014, our launch team was desperately seeking a location to plant our church in Oklahoma City, but we were struggling. One day as we were nearing Thanksgiving, I felt the Lord tell me to reach out to my brother and ask for forgiveness. After all, here I was, a church planter, but I harbored unforgiveness in my heart towards my own brother. I must admit, the conviction I felt was overwhelming. God knew that I needed to repair my current relationship before He could put me in charge of building new ones.

That day, I sent my brother a Facebook message, hoping I could reconnect with him. So great was the rift between us, that I didn't even have his phone number. Thankfully, he responded, and we established an open line of communication. The next steps were harder than a simple Facebook message. I had to humble myself and issue a vulnerable and heartfelt apology. I owned that my actions, years before, were immature and wrong. I had reacted out of emotion, behaved poorly, and regretted my reaction. I told him I was sorry. I shared about my difficulties in planting a new church in my city and how hypocritical I felt. I knew my struggle would go on until I was able to rebuild a relationship with him. Something in me died that day, something that *needed to die.*

Through the process of looking inward and recognizing my own failures as a brother, friend and Christ follower, God revealed hidden sin in my life, buried deep, but would have manifested itself in a much more tangible way if I had not dealt with it then. God knew my heart, better than I did. He used this terrible situation I caused to refine my life and draw me closer to Him.

As I wrote this section, I was reminded of a passage in the book of Numbers. The story of the Israelites, when the twelve spies who were sent out to survey the promised land returned. Only Joshua and Caleb gave a positive report and because of the ten who had given a negative report, Israel declined moving forward into the Promised Land.

So, God's chosen people waited, not only to possess their promised land, but their disbelief caused them to wait until their entire generation had died. God did not want His people to possess something they did not believe He was capable of giving them.[2]

I knew God had an amazing new church for my wife and I to lead. We were holding tightly to the vision God had for us. However, I realized that something in me had to die before we could move into that promise. Through the process of purifying and refining my heart, God revealed that you cannot lead well if you do not love well.

It has been my experience that God is just as concerned about what is going on in the life of a church planter as He is with the church being planted. That holds true for all of us as believers and any spiritual endeavor we attempt. As Christians, it is our responsibility to attempt to walk in love and harmony with the people in our lives.

After the initial connection through Facebook, during the week of Thanksgiving, my brother and I met up a few weeks later at a favorite pizza place in our hometown. After making the 15-hour drive to meet, I sat with my brother, talking, reconnecting, and rekindling our relationship; one that has since brought healing to other relationships in our family. I remain amazed, as I watch God continue to do incredible healing. As we continue to move forward, let's define and take an in-depth look at what forgiveness really is.

FORGIVENESS DEFINED

I think forgiveness can be a taboo topic that people avoid because everyone has been hurt by someone at some point in their lives. People say things that have crushed us, and they do things that break our hearts. So, why does God call us to forgive? First of all, let's address the elephant in the room with forgiveness. People don't want to forgive someone else because they don't want to let them off the hook.

When someone hurts us, it is ingrained in us because of our sin nature, to want that person to "get theirs". We want to see them pay for hurting us. It is all about the need for retribution, we want our offenders to pay, and pay dearly.

That is not what God wants for us, and it is not helpful. The purpose of forgiveness is not only about showing mercy to others, but also about allowing our own hearts to heal and be set free from the drain that vengeful thinking brings into our lives.

Pastor Peter Haas, the pastor of Substance Church in the Twin Cities in Minnesota, once said, "Forgiveness is not about letting someone off of the hook, it's about taking them off of your hook and putting them on God's hook."[3] In other words, forgiveness is about freeing you, so you no longer have to carry the weight of what happened.

Carrying unforgiveness towards someone is like allowing them to live rent free in your mind. There is no such thing as free rent, and the cost of footing the bill on unforgiveness is one that you cannot afford to pay. Allow yourself to evict the unforgiveness taking up residence in your heart.

No one is asking you to forget what happened. Forgiveness does not mean that things will return immediately to the way they were. Forgiveness is often given quickly, but moving forward, moving on, requires trust and that is earned back slowly. God created this process as a defense mechanism, a form of emotional atonement, to protect us.

Think about the first time you burned yourself on the stove and that memory is literally seared into you, what an unpleasant yet weighty example of how memory serves as a defense from future hurt. I still remember the day I found out burners just switched to the off position can still be hot; heat does not dissipate immediately, it lingers. The pain from that moment served as a lesson; one I cannot seem to forget. You see, no part of me wants to walk through that pain again, so I am thankful that I remember. Forgiving someone of their transgression is not the same as forgetting that it happened, our remembering is meant to be a protection for us. Imagine if someone were to shoot you in the chest, you would not take the gun and put it back in their hands to hurt you again. No one would expect you to do that, but forgiveness does require us to take people off **our** hook and place them on God's. To completely turn them over to Him.

THE FORGIVEN FORGIVE

Matthew 18 tells of a servant of the king who owed a large debt. It would have been the equivalent of hundreds of thousands of dollars today. The time came for the man to pay back his debt. However, he did not have the money. The man was brought before the king and it was ordered that he and his family, along with all they had, be sold to repay his debt. The man fell on his face before the king and begged for patience. Moved, the king completely forgave the man's debt. He stamped paid in full on the bill and let his servant go.

Imagine the weight lifted from that man, the excitement evident with every move. Leaving the palace, he must have been dancing in the streets like a scene out of *La La Land*. Elated that his debt had been forgiven, he went on his way, but then something happened. The servant stumbled upon a fellow who owed him a small sum, which would be a few hundred bucks for us.

Instantly, remembering the debt owed to him, he grabbed the man, began to choke him, and demanded payment. The second man could not repay him. Listen to what happened in verse 30, "But he refused. Instead, he went off and had the man thrown in prison until he could pay the debt."[4]

In the palace, other servants reported to the king what they had seen. Furious, he had the servant brought before him, saying, "You wicked servant. I canceled all that debt of yours because you begged me to. Shouldn't you have had mercy on your fellow servant just as I had on you?"[5] In anger, the king handed him over to the jailers to be tortured, until he should pay back all that he owed.

YOU CANNOT LEAD WELL IF YOU DON'T LOVE WELL

I share this story with you to remind you that the forgiven should forgive. The tale concludes by saying, "This is how my heavenly Father will treat each of you unless you forgive your brother or sister from your heart."[6]

Matthew 6:14-15 also says, "For if you forgive people when they sin against you, your heavenly father will forgive you. But if you do not forgive others their sins, your Father will not forgive your sins."[7]

If you want forgiveness for your missteps, then forgiving others is paramount. Do not let unforgiveness rob you of a life free from the millstone of blame. Practice forgiveness, forgive others and see how your perspective changes.

OLD SCHOOL FORGIVENESS

Years and years ago, there was a one-room schoolhouse that served the families of a small community. The class held upwards of 25 students, from a diverse variety of backgrounds. Some kids from wealthy families, some from middle-class families and a few came from poorer living conditions.

As the students entered the schoolhouse for their first day of school, they were greeted by their new teacher. After the students placed their things on a shelf across the room, they chose their desks and sat down. The new teacher introduced himself as Mr. Miller.

He said the first thing on the agenda for the day was to establish a list of classroom rules, an important thing for sure– and in this list of rules the students would determine the punishments.

As Mr. Miller began to call out the rules, he wrote them on a small blackboard at the front of the room and then asked students to suggest possible punishments for breaking each rule – everyone had to agree.

"What should happen when a student is late to school?" the teacher asked.

Mary, a sweet little girl in the front row, said, "A late student should have to stay after class and write sentences like – 'I won't be late to class again', or 'next time I will be to class on time'." The entire class chimed in and agreed that this was a good punishment for the first rule.

"How about when a student talks while the teacher is speaking? What type of punishment should there be?" Mr. Miller asked.

Eddy, a small blonde boy in the middle of the room said, "At first there should be a warning, and then after that they should have to clean the chalkboard and erasers after school." Everyone in the room agreed that this too was a good punishment.

"What are some other rules?" The teacher asked the class.

A voice from the back of the room squeaked out, "How about no fighting?"

Another voice blurted out, "How about no cheating on your school-work."

A third suggested, "No stealing from the school or other classmates."

"What kind of punishment should there be if any of these three rules are broken then?" the teacher asked the class.

Steve, a good-looking boy sitting on the right side yelled out, "Oh, these are bad things – there should be big punishments for fighting, cheating and stealing."

Other little voices began to agree and confirm what Steve had said, when another voice shouted out, "If these rules are broken, there should be spankings!"

A new little boy piped up and said, "Yeah, five hard spankings right in front of the class."

The hails of agreement grew louder and louder, to the point that the teacher had to calm them back down.

"Now, you understand that once these rules are made, they must be carried out fully?" asked Mr. Miller.

In due course, the class agreed that the rules were good, and that they should be implemented right away.

Days later, the students were all outside playing before lunch. Everyone, that is – except for Timmy. While the rest of the class was enjoying a good game during recess, Timmy had casually snuck back into the school room. He found himself in front of a shelf full of lunch bags – lunches that the students had packed and brought with them from home. Everyone knew that Timmy came from a poor family and that food was scarce in his house. He was skinny, dirty, poorly dressed, and many of the other kids knew Timmy's living conditions.

The class came in from recess and grabbed their lunches. As they sat down at their desks to eat, Billy, one of the biggest and strongest kids in the class shouted out, "My food is gone, someone ate my sandwich!"

The classroom got extremely quiet, and everyone stopped their eating. Mr. Miller went to the front to address the class. "Whoever took Billy's sandwich needs to get up right now and come to the front of the class. We will figure out who took this sandwich, and you will be punished. Now is the time to confess."

To everyone's surprise, Timmy – afraid and embarrassed – stood up and with sandwich smudges on his face. He made his way to the front of the classroom. "It was you, Timmy?" asked Mr. Miller.

Ashamed, the young boy nodded his head.

"Class, you know what has to be done don't you? A few weeks ago, we made a rule that anyone caught stealing would be punished."

The entire class was saddened about the rule. Sure, they wanted to see the rules upheld as much as anyone, but none wanted Timmy to get spanked. If anyone needed food, it was Timmy.

"But Mr. Miller," a little boy shouted from the back of the classroom. "We said that stealing was punishable by five spankings in front of the class, but we never said that the person who was caught stealing had to be the one to take the spankings."

Mr. Miller scratched his head and looked at the blackboard where he had written the rules and punishments weeks previous. "You are absolutely right," said Mr. Miller. "But is there anyone who would choose to take Timmy's place?"

At that moment, in the back of the classroom, Billy stood up. Thoughts of panic raced through Timmy's head as the biggest kid, the one whose sandwich he had taken, was making his way down the center aisle, toward the front of the classroom.

Shocked and surprise rained down as Billy spoke, "I will – I'll take Timmy's place. I'll take the five spankings."

UNTHINKABLE LOVE

No one present in the classroom that day ever expected anyone else would step up and take the punishment for Timmy. After all, he was the one who had broken the rules and though some were broken-hearted for him, they knew he had to pay the price.

Until Billy, a most unlikely ally decided to stand up and come forward. Can you believe it? The very one who had his lunch taken was the one who traded places with Timmy.

In much the same way, no one anticipated that Jesus would step in and take the punishment for the sins of the world. He was the most unlikely person, being the Son of God, the one we had wronged with our sin. Yet, it was His **unthinkable** love that moved Him to step in for us.

When we harbor unforgiveness, the only person that we are harming is ourselves. As Jeanne Mayo often says, "Bitterness is like swallowing poison and hoping that someone else dies."[8] That is crazy, right? If you drink poison, it is only going to kill you! And the reality is that unforgiveness does not hurt the offender at all, it only adds hurt and pain to your life.

How wonderful is it that God does not hold our offenses against us like we typically do with others? Instead, Romans 5:8 says, "...while we were yet sinners, Christ died for us."[9] In our lives we should work to forgive freely like God has done for us. As we release others by forgiving them, we are following Jesus' example and releasing ourselves into God's love and forgiveness. His *unthinkable* love.

I like to put it this way; our willing act of forgiveness toward others opens the door for us to freely receive the gift of forgiveness that God is extending to us.

THE FRUIT OF FORGIVENESS

In Luke 19, Jesus tells Zacchaeus that he wants to go back to his house and spend time with him. When the local people hear this, they call out against it, and then Zac turns to Jesus, and he tells him, "Look, Lord! Here and now I give half of my possessions to the poor, and if I have cheated anybody out of anything, I will pay back four times the amount."[10]

We see the fruit of forgiveness already taking shape in Zacchaeus' life. He is willing to right all his wrongs while seeking out forgiveness. As Jesus looks at Zac, He offers these life changing words, "Today, salvation has come to this house."[11] We need reminding that the beauty of forgiveness is found once you have learned to forgive, and that can change people's lives forever.

Start challenging yourself to do the *unthinkable* and forgive easily. With time, forgiveness will become less of a struggle and the anger and bitterness of old hurts will fade. Forgiveness is a choice, and the choice is yours. It may not be what you feel like doing, and unforgiveness may feel justified, but it will never bring a win to your life. So, learn to take the right steps in forgiving others and as you do, the unrivaled love of God will engulf your life. That is the beauty of forgiveness.

FIELD NOTES

KEY IDEAS:

- You cannot lead well if you do not love well!
- Forgiveness is not about letting someone else off the hook, but it is about setting your own heart free.
- Bitterness is like swallowing poison and hoping that someone else dies.

FOLLOW-UP QUESTIONS:

1. What needs to die inside of you so that God's plan and purpose for your life can thrive?
3. Have you ever practiced forgiveness with someone else? How did it turn out?
5. Who do you need to forgive today? Is there anyone you need forgiveness from, right now?

FIELD
NOTES

GIVE GENEROUSLY

CHAPTER FIVE · CHAPTER FIVE · CHAPTER FIVE · CHAPTER FIVE · CHAPTER FIVE · CHAPTER FIVE · CHAPTER FIVE

Another way you can live that is absolutely *unthinkable* to the world around you is to be a person who gives generously. This will seem odd, crazy even, but to God, it serves as a vital part of what a daily walk with Him looks like. If you look at the examples laid out in the Bible, one thing to note is that God gives generous people influence.

Everyone loves a giver, especially when they are giving to you or to your cause, but what it takes to be a giver is often difficult. Although when God is the one asking, it can turn out to mean something entirely unexpected.

ABRAHAM'S TEST

When I think of what giving looked like in the Bible, I cannot help but turn to the incredible story of Abraham and his son Isaac. The story is one of immense sacrifice by today's standards, a truly *unthinkable* encounter. Genesis 22 opens with a test. Abraham, now more than 100-years-old, has been promised by God that his descendants would become more numerous than the grains of sand on the earth. However, things take a shift and do not go like Abraham thought they were going to. As we read on, God requires that Abraham take his only one legitimate son, up a mountain and sacrifice him there. This doesn't add up though, does it? A man who was more than 100-years-old is probably not going to have any more children, and God asking Abraham to sacrifice Isaac, seems like it might put a kink in the plan. It will be a major roadblock to the promise God made about Abraham having countless descendants. To Abraham's relief, God reveals that He was not asking for sacrifice as much as He desired Abraham's obedience. In fact, that is really what our giving is about.

In the end, God provided a substitute sacrifice, spared Isaac's life, and fulfilled His promise to Abraham. God does not need our sacrifices, although He delights in them, much like a parent who finds pleasure in something made by their child. What He takes joy in more than sacrifice, is in our obedience to His commands and our willingness to do what He asks us. God loves to see our obedience and then to bless it.

We can look to other scriptures to see more of God's response to obedience. In Malachi chapter 3:10-11 it says, "'Bring the whole tithe into the storehouse, that there may be food in my house. Test me in this,' says the Lord Almighty, 'and see if I will not throw open the floodgates of heaven and pour out so much blessing that there will not be room enough to store it.'"[1]

Within Christianity today, we can interpret the storehouse as our local church. It is the place where we go for spiritual teaching, growth, and edification. Thinking of it as a storehouse can help us visualize how our generosity is used for God's kingdom and purpose. The modern-day church functions as a storehouse much the same as when Joseph set up a place to stockpile, and later dispense, the grain during the famine in Egypt. This storehouse for Pharaoh was eventually used to help keep the people from starvation.[2] We bring our tithes and our offerings, pooling them so that funds are available for weekly ministry, benevolence, and outreach, doing more joined together than they could separately.

When we are generous with our finances, it is an act of worship. This comes from a heart of obedience, and it is a result of adopting a posture of faith in our daily lives. When giving our tithes and offerings, we are trusting God and acknowledging where our true resources come from. It is just as much of an outward sign of our continued walk with God as prayer or regular church attendance is. Why do so many have difficulty in this act of obedience? Why is giving our tithes and offerings living in the *unthinkable*?

It takes faith.

Hebrews 11:6 says, "Without faith it is impossible to please God."[3] Our giving requires a great deal of faith on our part. Ask anyone who has a standard worldview, and they will tell you that it seems *unthinkable* to give ten percent of your income to the church, to God's storehouse.

For many who have not experienced the miracle of the tithe, there is often fear of the unknown. If you were barely making it with 100 percent of your income, how can you live on just 90 percent after you tithe?

I agree with Kevin Ward, a friend and fellow pastor, when he said, "I would rather live on 90 percent with God's blessing, than 100 percent without it." Your accountant cannot explain it but giving God the ten percent tithe is our obedient step of faith and shows trust in God as our provider.

I want to encourage you to step out and trust God with your resources. As you walk deeper into relationship with God, you will be perplexed and astounded that the 90/10 life is not only possible, but it will also become a best practice, and one you will want to share with others.

The reality is we cannot out-give God! No matter your income, your resources, your sacrifice, it is just not possible to out-give the creator of the world. In fact, I dare you to try. It's just not possible.

At various points in our lives, we all have had to come face-to-face with the part our money and possessions play in our daily struggles and successes. Each one of us, on some level, has a relatively good idea of what we spend our money on. The older we get, the clearer our spending habits can become. Some costs grow larger, like medical bills or prescriptions, and others become fixed in place, like a mortgage payment. If talking about finances normally bothers you, please, read through this chapter with an open mind, and a ready heart. Take a few minutes to pray that God will give you insights to your own financial future and help you look at your own choices through His eyes. Give a critical once over to your expenses and allow God to refine you in this area, as he has in others.

In the Bible, prayer is discussed 500 times and faith approximately the same amount. However, it has nearly 2,000 scriptures about our money and possessions. God knows the grip money and things can have over us.

Allowing God dominion over our worldly possessions is an important step towards complete surrender, where He can search us and speak into anything in our lives.

I write this, not as a pastor, but as a fellow follower of Jesus who wants you to know that this is **big news** and that it **works**. There is someone you know that sells a product of some sort. You've seen their Facebook promotions. You've read their testimonials. You've been handed an invite to their next party, and they have zero shame talking to you about something they love and are passionate about. I'm here to tell you that I am passionate about this principle of trusting God with your generosity. The miracles I have experienced in my life are direct results of these acts of obedience, specifically in giving. Generosity has changed my life and enhanced my purpose. Throughout the rest of this chapter, I want to share with you some of those stories of obedience. My earnest hope is that as you read through my own faith-experiences you will come to see why I feel so passionate about this topic. Stepping into generosity in your walk as a Jesus follower is not about what God wants from you, but it is about what God wants for your life.

OUR STORY

In late Summer of 2009, we welcomed our son, Asher "Ryan" Wardwell, into our family. In our married life, there has been no greater joy than having and raising our children, Kierstyn and Ryan. Psalm 127:3 resonates with me when the Psalmist writes, "Children are a heritage from the Lord, offspring a reward from him. Like arrows in the hands of a warrior are children born in one's youth. Blessed is the man whose quiver is full of them."[4] My children are a majestic testament to my continued relationship with God, so much so that this book is dedicated to them.

Just after Ryan had turned one, in September of 2010, we were holding revival services with Lynn Wheeler at Central Assembly of God in Enid, Oklahoma. The weekend was filled with worship and ministry. We were all praying in the altar as the service came to an end. I can distinctly remember saying to myself how thankful I was for the season of life we were in.

While at the altar that evening, I knelt there, reflecting on the blessings in my life, and all I could do was thank God for his faithfulness and provision. He had carried us through the troubles of the 2007 housing market crash, allowing us to juggle a mortgage and rent for almost 2 years, and then giving us a new home in Enid just before Ryan was born. We were blessed with a home we loved, two precious children and our student ministry was growing. I felt I was at a very healthy place in my walk with God. So, it came as a surprise when my wife found me and with a tear-stained face told me she had made some mistakes.

In a moment like that, the greatest fears your mind can muster begin to play out, wreaking mental havoc similarly to a deafening roar like a jet engine with the afterburners on.

I was completely caught off guard. The Holy Spirit whispered to my heart, and I heard Him say, *"How you treat what she is about to tell you will forever impact your relationship and the direction of your marriage. Be careful!"*

So as the storm raged in my mind, I focused on the words of the Holy Spirit. I stilled the chaos within me, and I braced myself for what she was about to share.

This is humbling to admit, but I have not always been as compassionate and understanding in the past as God had prepared me to be in that moment. We are all works in progress, but, having married young, the survival in our first few years of marriage is due in large part to the commitment Kate had to fight for us. In our early years, it was her patience and consistency that bolstered us and moved us through difficult times. If there are awards in heaven for showing love and grace to an immature spouse, Kate would sit at the pinnacle of the Olympic podium. So, you can understand her hesitancy that night in sharing the mistake she had made.

Standing there together, at the altar, I froze and listened. She went on to tell me she had made some financial errors.

All throughout our marriage, Kate has paid the bills. She signs the back of our paychecks and deposits them. In the past, we joked that if I ever endorsed my own paycheck, I would be arrested for forgery. As a married couple, we each had agreed upon responsibilities, and managing our finances was one of hers. You readers who are married know exactly what I am talking about.

Since 2005, Kate has owned and operated her own graphic design business. She does it all, from bringing in business, to meeting deadlines, to sending final invoices to clients. It being her world, she knows what comes in and what goes out, and she has always managed her books effectively.

After baby number two, we experienced something new in our marriage. Kate began to have difficulties in her everyday interactions. She found herself struggling through a clouded headspace. Where her norm was quick-wittedness, now she was making small mistakes, missing payments, and acting out of character. She signed up for store credit cards to save money on back-to-school clothes for the kids, something she would not have done in the past.

Constantly overwhelmed and feeling lost within herself, Kate was experiencing what we learned was postpartum depression. She had never felt this way before. It had not happened with our first child, or earlier in her life, so Kate had no frame of reference for what it all meant. Out of fear of disappointing me, she tried to fix it on her own. Not realizing her emotions were eclipsing her normally superb judgment, she fell deeper and deeper into debt. Her depression had allowed things to spiral so profoundly, that the night she came to me at the altar she could not tell me how deep we were in debt. She just knew that we were. After looking at all the statements and bills together, we were more than $9,000 in debt.

I know that to some that does not sound like a lot of money. Throughout our lives we had worked hard to be good stewards. We both graduated without any college debt. We would only buy things on cards if we had the cash in hand to pay them back immediately. We had zero consumer debt. We did all of this so we could live generously and be givers. Finding ourselves in any amount of debt was a completely foreign occurrence. $9,000 of debt felt like Everest.

Obeying the Holy Spirit, I hugged my wife, I prayed for her, and I told her I knew in my heart that we were going to get through this and come out better on the other side. I didn't know how, but the words the Holy Spirit had whispered gave me comfort and challenged me to allow this situation to strengthen us and not push us apart.

I have always been taught that if you are in debt the best thing to do is to increase your giving. Give more away and live with less essentially. At that point in my life, with the amount of debt looming, it didn't make sense, but we felt like anything was worth a shot.

After talking it through and praying about it, Kate and I decided to do the **unthinkable** and we made a missions faith promise that was bigger than we had ever made before – and we got to work paying down our debt.

We first took any cash and put it directly towards debt. Then we consolidated the rest down to the cards with the lowest interest rates and began to make payments on those. We streamlined our monthly expenses, eliminating anything we could. For example, we turned off cable television and had date nights on the cheap. Instead of going to the movies, we rented a Redbox and microwaved a bag of popcorn. We took on a mantle of what Dave Ramsey's Financial Peace University calls, "Gazelle Intensity". At the same time each month even though it did not make sense from the outside, we would write our tithe and missions checks. We were determined to knock out our debt. In the process, we found out that you cannot out-give God.

Month after month we had exactly what we needed. Money came from places we never expected, and we were able to pay a sizable amount directly towards debt. Work flooded in for Kate. In December, someone gave so that we could buy Christmas presents for our kids. We were given money to travel home and see family. Our kids had clothes, a warm home to live in and food to eat. We felt utterly blessed!

As of January of 2011, just five months after Kate came to me at church and told me about our obstacle, we made our final credit card payment and were back in the black. We never stopped tithing. We never missed a missions giving opportunity. AND we never went without. This was a miracle our family will never forget. When we as followers of Jesus give God control of our finances, He provides for us. It might seem counterintuitive, or even appear crazy, but I have seen with my own eyes the miracles from God when we put our trust in Him - not just with our words, but with our finances.

LUNCH MONEY

When I was in elementary school there were a couple of ladies that I grew to love. Their names were Cheryl Ferrell and Betty Arrendale. These two ladies were special, they were two of our school's lunch ladies who thought I was a sweet boy and who gave me extra tater tots and chicken nuggets when I came through their lines. These ladies made sure I was well fed and could finish out my school day strong. In a word, I thought they were awesome.

Each day, as I left the house for school, my mom would give me a dollar bill for lunch that I would tuck into my sock. Yep, like many of my classmates that is how I carried my money back then – even though it proved a challenge when I had gym class before lunch. That is a different story for a different day.

I remember with a sense of nostalgia that ninety-five cents bought a full school lunch back then and I felt like I was rolling in the dough as I stocked up all those leftover nickels all year long. I would save them up to buy pencils and erasers at the yearly book fair. Ah, those were the days.

In the book of John, there is a story in chapter 6 that chronicles a young boy who was given what I like to think of as lunch money, only his destination was not the school cafeteria. The Bible does not give many details about the boy. We know neither his name, nor what became of him after encountering Jesus. He might have been headed to the marketplace, as the story opens directly before the Jewish Passover Festival, but it is unsure. However, we do know as he walked home on this particular day, he passed by a hill covered with people and a lot of commotion.

If this story had taken place in our time, as people were piling up on the hillside, Jesus might have been brainstorming with His disciples about the box lunches that were never delivered for the conference. Man, they would have marveled at a catered box meal from Chick-Fil-A! Can we just take a minute and thank the Lord for their warm chocolate chip cookies?

In that time things were different, there were no fast-food restaurants, or even consistent grocery stores. Most food was what we call farm-to-table or bartered for at local markets. With that in mind, Jesus asked Phillip, where can we get food for all these people?

Let us put ourselves in Phillip's place for a moment. Not only was he concerned about the amount of food, but after some quick calculations he figured the cost to give each person one bite of food would take a year's worth of wages. Philip was no doubt at a loss and a bit panicky.

In the face of similarly dire circumstances, I think we have all felt the weight and pressure of things that were out of our control. Lord, how am I going to make this month's rent payment? How am I going to finish this degree if I cannot pass this class? As a single parent, how am I going to provide everything for my kids that I need to? How can I move forward with my diagnosis? Life often places these sorts of hard questions in our path, and it is how we choose to respond and where we put our trust that makes the difference.

We see a slightly different response from Andrew, Simon Peter's brother, when he showed up in the story with the little boy holding a sack lunch. God often chooses to use those who are closest to Him. I seriously doubt it was a coincidence that they found the little boy walking past the hill that afternoon. It was providence because Jesus had a plan.

Before Jesus asked Phillip about the food, before Andrew spoke up, the story tells us that Jesus already had a plan in mind. So, when Andrew spoke to Jesus saying, "Here is a boy with five small barley loaves and two small fish, but how far will they go among so many?"[5] Jesus knew what the miracle He planned to perform would look like.

This whole set up begs the question – did Jesus need the boy's lunch that day? After all, God has been known to make food appear out of nowhere. In Exodus 16, God rained down manna from heaven that sustained the wandering Israelites for years. He also provided them with massive amounts of quail.[6] In another story, God sent ravens bearing food to feed a starving prophet in the wilderness.[7] So, did Jesus really need this young boy's food? Throughout His time on earth, Jesus taught His followers using many tools. This time, He wanted to show His disciples that when you are willing to give what you have, God loves to make you part of the miracle. God loves when we are close enough to Him that He can include us in His story.

When you grow in relationship with someone else, you become a part of their life, a part of their story. In much the same way, when we find ourselves in step with God and drawing closer to Him each day, He includes us in his story, in his plans, in doing the *unthinkable*. Once something is placed in God's hands, it can do more, and go so much farther than when it remains in our hands. In our hands, even the choicest of things never reach the apex of their potential, but in God's hands He can use even the most mundane to do miracles.

It's a lot like a basketball. Although I grew up in Indiana and I love the game, a basketball, in my hands is only worth about 30 bucks. While a basketball in Russell Westbrook's or Steph Curry's hand is worth millions.

To carry the illustration further, a paintbrush in my hand is not impressive at all, but paintings by the hand of Vincent van Goh are priceless, and on display in museums of art around the globe. Equally, I enjoy cooking and eating as much as anyone, but none would pay a large amount to eat something I've whipped up in the kitchen, but a six-course ensemble put together by Emeril Lagasse or Tom Douglas would be a meal fit for a king and cost a king's ransom as well. My point is, in most cases, the potential of something is tied to the hands that are holding it. In our story, the five loaves and two fish were taken from the young boy and given into the hands of Jesus, the Messiah, the Savior of the world, the Son of God.

As Jesus stood, holding the little boy's lunch in His hands the Bible says He, "… took it, He blessed it, He broke it, and He handed it back so that the disciples could distribute it." In my experience, when God requests something from you, He has every intention of giving it back.

GENEROSITY IS NOT ABOUT WHAT GOD WANTS FROM YOU, BUT WHAT GOD WANTS FOR YOU

The miracle comes when you decide to relinquish control and surrender it to Him. He then blesses it and puts it back, made better than it was before. If we desire to see the hands of God move, to watch Him do the miraculous with our meager gifts, we must first learn to give them and freely place them in His outstretched hands.

MORE THAN MONEY

Living a generous life is about more than money. Yes, in many situations what we give is out of our wallets and purses, but God is looking for more than our earthly treasures. The way you marshal your time, and your talents also impact your level of generosity. Outside of our financial resources, God is also asking us to look at our calendars and He's expecting us to make time for Him in our schedules.

Time is a precious commodity for certain, but one that everyone has an equal amount of each day. We all get 24 hours, 1,440 minutes, 86,400 seconds – however you want to calculate it. We all have the same amount of time each day! How are you budgeting it? How much time are you giving to God? Ephesians 5:15-16 reminds us to, "…be careful how you walk, not as unwise men but as wise, making the most of your time, because the days are evil."[8]

We have all heard the phrase, "Life happens" and if we are not careful, the hours can turn from days to weeks and before our eyes, life slips away. If we allow ourselves to, we can become so busy living our lives that we forget who we are living for.

I hope you realize that you were born for a specific purpose. Your gifts and talents are unique and are valuable within the community of believers you do life with. Paul said it this way in 1 Corinthians 12:7, "A spiritual gift is given to each of us so we can help each other."[9] In other words, God has blessed you with a gifting the people around you need. Paul goes on to elaborate what some of those gifts are. Some have the gift of encouragement, some have a gift of faith, some have a gift of prophecy and others a gift of praying for the sick to be healed. He gives a whole list of them. The chapter continues with a list of these gifts that are manifested through the Spirit of God in the lives of believers. These gifts range in variety. All of these are given as the Holy Spirit decides. Just as a body has many different parts and all are needed, you have a talent that is needed in the body of Christ as well. When we are generous with our time and talents, God can use our lives and abilities in much the same way as He uses our giving. God wants us to give Him the trifecta of our time, talents, and treasures and in doing that, yield the fruit in our lives that He is cultivating and developing in and through us.

MAKING ROOM FOR MORE

In 2 Kings 4, there is a story about a widow who has been burdened with her deceased husband's debt.[10] We are not given many details about the origin of the debt, or the circumstances of the debtor's death, but the story opens as the wife calls on Elisha for advice and help.

The woman pleaded with Elisha to tell her what to do to prevent the creditors from taking her two sons and selling them into slavery to repay the debt.

Elisha inquired what possessions the woman had. After hearing she had only a jar of oil to her name, Elisha gave her these instructions: "Go around and ask all your neighbors for empty jars. Don't ask for just a few." He continued, "...pour oil into all the jars, and as each is filled, put it to one side."[11]

The woman did just as Elisha said, and her sons brought her jars to fill as she poured the oil from her jar into the borrowed ones. When all the jars were full, and her sons assured her there were no more, the oil stopped flowing from her jar. At this, she returned to the man of God, and Elisha told her to sell the oil, pay her debts and live on the excess proceeds.

I wonder what was going through that woman's mind as she filled the final jar. What would have happened if she had found a dozen more jars? What about fifty more? One hundred more? Beyond paying off her debt, she could have purchased a new home, bought livestock, or sent her son for an apprenticeship.

The oil only stopped flowing because the woman ran out of room to pour it. God filled the jars until there was no more room. In the same way, God is looking at our lives and seeking space to pour, but He cannot exceed the margin we give Him. Just like the oil God will not continue allowing His presence to overflow if we live miserly and avoid the life of generosity as He desires. When we do not give the Lord space, our jars will remain filled with all the wrong things. As we empty ourselves, giving of our time, talents, and treasures, our lives become a reflection of God. We must not be so full of ourselves that there is no room for Jesus. The apostle John said it best when he said, "He must become greater, I must become less."[12]

THE TRUTH ABOUT SEEDS

One last thing that I want to share with you on this subject that will make you and your actions **unthinkable** to the people around you is called, "The Law of Sowing and Reaping."

Farmers and investors alike are familiar with the law of sowing and reaping. Both on the farm and Wall Street, there is an understanding that you cannot draw out what you have not put in. During harvest time, there is only a crop if during planting season, the soil was plowed, and seeds were sown. Savvy investors only receive returns when investments are made, when their money is placed in stock or bonds and allowed to grow. Within the law, there are rules when nothing is ventured, nothing is gained. The farmer is giving up his seed and the investor their money in hopes that they will see a return on that investment.

We see a promise about the way God treats returns on investment in His kingdom in Luke 6:38, "Give, and it will be given to you. A good measure, pressed down, shaken together, and running over, will be poured into your lap. For with the measure you use, it will be measured to you."[13] God wants us to live generously and remember that the law of sowing and reaping extends to His kingdom and our daily purpose within it.

I will never forget the story of Ronald Wayne. He was one of Apple's three co-founders. Sure, you have heard of Steve Job's and Steve Wozniak, but Wayne is one that was left out of the history books.

Who was this Ronald Wayne and why has his name been lost over time? In 1976, just 12 days after the birth of the company, Wayne got cold feet and renounced his part ownership of the company. His investment at that time was about $800. If he had not cashed and instead retained his position, as of the summer of 2021 his shares would have been worth almost 63 billion dollars.[14]

Giving to God is neither a crapshoot nor a gamble. God's economy is not like our economy. The understanding that God's economy is perfect like He is, makes the investment of generosity through your time, talent, and treasure more than worth the effort. We must remember that when it comes to sowing into God's kingdom, there will be eternal dividends, so we cannot lose.

FIELD NOTES

KEY IDEAS:

- I would rather live on 90 percent with God's blessing, than 100 percent without it.
- Things in God's hands turn out better than when they are left in mine.
- When it comes to your time, your talents, and your treasures, know that you cannot out-give God.

FOLLOW-UP QUESTIONS:

1. If you take an inventory, what do you spend most of your money on? (No judgment here, just an honest question.)
2. If you could help someone else with your giving, would you?
3. Do you trust your local church to use the tithes and offerings you give appropriately, so that together you can make a difference in others' lives?

CHALLENGE:

If you have never leaned-in to tithing, I want to challenge you to step out and see what God will do with your faithfulness. Watch and see what happens next as you patiently trust Him.

FIELD NOTES

CHAPTER SIX · CHAPTER SIX · CHAPTER SIX · CHAPTER SIX · CHAPTER SIX · CHAPTER SIX · CHAPTER SIX · CHAPTER SIX ·

SERVE
SACRIFICIALLY

³Do nothing out of selfish ambition or vain conceit. Rather, in humility value others above yourselves, ⁴not looking to your own interests but each of you to the interests of the others.

Philippians 2:3-4

Part of God's plan for us, and another way to live an **unthinkable** life for Jesus, is to serve others sacrificially. God's heartbeat is for us to serve one another.

Jesus told his disciples in Mark 9:35 that if any of them wanted to be great in the kingdom then they were going to have to learn how to serve each other.[1] He even went to great lengths in John 13 to set an example as He took a towel, wrapped it around His waist, and took the position of the lowest servant in the house by kneeling down and washing the disciples' feet.[2]

Jesus' example reminds us that He wants our faith to be in action. We should seek people and opportunities to serve and pour our lives out for. The life of a person who has decided to follow Jesus is marked by an attitude and lifestyle of service. In other words, as I always like to say – saved people serve people.

THE EXTRA MILE

Matthew 5:41 says, "If anyone forces you to go one mile, go with them two miles."[3] In the time that Jesus and His disciples walked the streets of Jerusalem, the city was under the rule of the Roman Empire and it was a law that if a Roman soldier asked a Jewish citizen to carry his rucksack that he had to carry it at least one mile - no questions asked.

In this passage, Jesus is simply telling His followers they should make the effort to go the extra mile (literally) and offer to carry it for two. The same rings true today. As followers of Christ, we are challenged to go above and beyond for others.

If you have ever attempted something that requires skill for the first time, you know that often there are specialized guides offering direction, or a safety net along the way. For skydiving, a guide will co-dive with you for your first few jumps. With scuba diving, a similar instructor will walk you through the experience before you go in too deep. For those climbing Everest there are special servants called *Sherpas*. On Kilimanjaro, they are referred to as *porters*. These are the people who basically make it possible to reach the top.

The porters of Kilimanjaro are local Tanzanians, and they carry several bags up the mountain that many could never lug up to the summit. Our porter, though small in stature, was exceptionally fit, and able to make the same journey as us while carrying most of our gear. Porters carried our food, tent, sleeping bags and other important items. More than just helping with the load, while on the mountain they set up tents, prepared meals, and kept us company while hiking. These men are amazing individuals with a servant's heart, and they make getting to Uhuru Peak, the highest point in Africa, a possibility.

Below you will find an excerpt from day four of my climb that describes our porters and what they did to serve us and help us get to the top:

KILIMANJARO: BARAFU CAMP
THURSDAY, SEPTEMBER 19TH, 2013

We woke up as usual by packing our tent, and then we washed our hands in the water that Doddi had warmed up for us, then we slipped into the mess tent for breakfast. By now, we were tired of African wilderness food. We loved the people who prepared it, but not the food itself. We headed to Karanga from Baranco camp. It was full of ups and downs. Some of the most beautiful views I have ever seen and some of the hardest technical climbs. When we left Baranco camp we took what was known as "Baranco Wall". Nate loved it, but it freaked me out. There were several of those "whoops, good-bye" parts. The kind your mom would not like to know about. Other than the wall, the trip was pretty simple and awesome. We ran into a young man from Berlin. His dad started the trip with him but got sick, so he went back down. It happens a lot on the mountain. At this point, those who started at Macheme are being weeded out.

We got to Karanga. It was literally a pad on a hill in the middle of the valley and we were sitting ducks for any bad storms. Clouds were rolling in. So, we decided to press on for Barafu. The name Barafu in Swahili means, "ice'. It was fitting that as we walked up to the camp it was sleeting and cold. Now at more than 15,000 feet we were poised for the summit. We waited for our tent to be set up in the shelter of Barafu hut. Once our tent was ready, we ate and then went straight to bed. 5AM was going to come quickly.

Tomorrow is summit day!

As you could see from the excerpt in my journal, the porters were an incredible help. They warmed the water for us, set up our tents and made our beds. They carried our supplies and made us comfortable. Getting us to the top of Kilimanjaro and back home alive was the win for them.

Have you ever stopped to realize that when we serve others and we help them win, that we win? I want us to dive into some stories where individuals lived lives of service towards others, with their goal being to reflect the love of Jesus and guide others to Him.

ANOTHER TAX COLLECTOR

As we move into the story in Matthew 9, I would like to paint a picture for you, envisioning what the experience might have been like. While the Bible does not go into detail about every part of this meeting between Jesus and Matthew, we can imagine it together.[4]

I can see Matthew working away on some paperwork when Jesus comes up to the booth where he spent his days collecting taxes. It was uncommon for people to just visit Matthew by choice. Even today, tax collectors do not have the best reputation. However, in Roman times, they were known for being corrupt and crooked people who preyed on the overtaxed populace and lined their pockets. Matthew looked up, as Jesus calmly approached him while he sat at his table, finishing up and getting ready to close for the day. Jesus' arrival really caught him off guard. Turning from his papers, Matthew looked up, and exchanged a long look with Jesus of Nazareth, the man he had heard of before but never personally met.

Jesus' reputation preceded him, and a smile came across Matthew's face.

We do not know the full extent of the exchange between Jesus and Matthew that day. I wish we knew the conversation and what all was said, but all we have recorded are just the two words of Jesus, "Follow Me". Maybe that's the point. Maybe the call of Jesus is that simple, that we should lay everything aside, even when we don't have a well laid out plan or all the details in front of us. Again, Jesus said, "Follow me". He didn't demand it, He did not try to convince Matthew, and yet that day things were set in motion in Matthew's life.

As we move on in the story from the initial encounter with Jesus, we see that Matthew has invited many people, his friends, and colleagues over to meet Jesus and have dinner together. So that night, when Jesus showed up to Matthew's house for dinner, the house was filled with people.

Can you imagine how unnerving this must have been for Matthew? Meeting with the Son of God would have been overwhelming to say the least. If entering the presence of God in worship today gives us any indication, the feeling of being so close to the physical human embodiment of the Living God must have been amazing. I like to believe that Matthew was overwhelmingly taken with the holiness apparent in Jesus' every action. So much so, that he went around for the rest of the day trying to get people to meet Him, to also experience what must have been a surreal encounter filled with peace and joy.

So, Matthew, having gathered as many friends and coworkers as he could, filled his household and dined with Jesus. If you seek out opportunities for the *unthinkable* in your walk with God, then serving others is not only a logical next step but can lead to yet another *unthinkable* action, introducing others to Jesus. Matthew is not the only one who was so changed by their encounter with Jesus that they wanted to share it with the world. As we continue, we are going to hone in on other stories where Jesus and His followers modeled the *unthinkable* in their everyday lives.

Let us examine a group of four men that helped a friend get an audience with Jesus. A group of people who did the *unthinkable*. They were willing to do whatever it took to gain access to Jesus. I alluded to this story at the start of this book, but now, we can take a closer look.

GRAB A CORNER

News about the miracle man, the wise teacher, Jesus, traveled fast. Today, the hum and buzz from Capernaum was that He was in a nearby house teaching and praying for the sick. Living in a small house just down the street was a paralytic man. It is unclear how long this man had been afflicted, and we aren't brought in on many of the details of the situation. We are never told if he was in a tragic accident or if he had been this way since birth. All we know is that his need was great, and he was desperate.

Matthew 9 says that there were some men in his life that stepped up in a big way. We don't exactly know this connection either, but I cannot help but think these men were good friends. If they were not close before this day, they definitely were when it was all over. The story tells us that these men each grabbed a corner of his bed and they carried him right out of the door toward the place where Jesus was.[5]

GOD'S HEART BEAT IS FOR US TO SERVE ONE ANOTHER

However, when the men came closer to the house, they saw something that stopped them in their tracks and caught them off guard – people were everywhere. The house was standing room only. In fact, the massive crowd spilled out into the front yard and down the street. It was like a scene you have probably seen before in a movie or on television where CNN, Fox News, and all the major local news channels are swarming someone's yard. In the same way, people were everywhere listening to Jesus teach.

For me, when things do not go as planned, I have some major problems. I like to be in control, to settle things in my mind and see them play-out just so. Often, I will lie awake at night planning out my tomorrow, how the meeting is going to go – and I find myself disappointed when it does not happen like I planned it. The mat carriers probably felt like that. They were left wondering, "What in the world are we supposed to do?"

They could have turned around and left in defeat saying, "Well, it was worth a shot, we can try again the next time." That is not what happened, though. Faced with such a situation, they did not give up like you might expect. The men, instead of seeing the situation as a lost cause, choose to look at the obstacle from a different angle. They didn't back down, they doubled down.

We are once again not given a lot of detail describing what the next moments must have been like, but as Jesus was speaking there suddenly came a strange sound on the roof – the sound of footsteps. Sure enough, the team of four men worked together, used creativity, and somehow were able to get their paralytic friend and his mat up on the roof.

As Jesus was speaking to the crowd, clumps of dirt and dust began to fall from the ceiling. The Pharisees and everyone listening must have been wondering what in the world was going on! Our paralytic friend and his entourage decided to cut through the dirt and thatch roof of the house and before you know it, they begin to lower their friend down from the ceiling.

People in the house squeezed together and moved aside to avoid the falling ceiling as a man on a mat was lowered down to the floor.

As the man on the mat gently touched down at His feet, Jesus remained unfazed by all of it. In Mark's gospel account, he makes sure to tell us that Jesus noticed the faith of the group of men. Jesus looked up through the new skylight in the ceiling and noted the faith of the four who brought their friend and lowered him down. He saw their faith and willingness to do whatever it would take to get their friend to Jesus. It was by their faith that the man on the mat was made whole.

I love this story because what these men did for their friend was utterly **unthinkable** and exceptionally bold. I want to challenge you with a hard question today, will you take a corner of someone's mat and go the extra mile to get them to Jesus? Even with walls and obstacles in your way, will you dig through and do something **unthinkable** to get them to Jesus, the one who can truly meet their every need?

Now, it is implied by the law that the next day someone was going to have to go back and patch up the roof where the miracle had taken place. After all, the law states that whatever you did to someone else, you had to make it right. If you killed their ox, you had to give them one of yours. If you took out their eye, you had to allow them to put out yours. "Eye for an eye, tooth for a tooth, life for a life."[6] Someone had to go back and repair that roof, right? I love it. Yesterday there were four men climbing up on top of the roof, but today there were five.

Today the miracle happens to you, so that tomorrow the miracle can happen through you!

Remember, there are no better poster children of God's love and grace than those who have just been shown it. There are no greater publicity agents for Jesus than those who have personally encountered Him. We worship a God who is alive, whose handiwork can be seen throughout our lives, and He has a plan and a purpose for each one of his children. Sometimes that plan includes grabbing a corner for someone else and walking them to Jesus and to their healing. We all have a responsibility to tell our story to others and to get them to Jesus.

TELL THE SECRET

There was a slave who lived in the south during the Civil War era. One night, after an altercation with the plantation owner and years of abuse, the slave decided that he could no longer abide these brutal conditions. The meager meals, intensely rigorous labor, and relentless physical abuse had pushed him to his limits. He found himself at his breaking point and could not endure it anymore.

He had heard tales of other men and women, similarly afflicted, and how they had broken free from their tyrannical overseers and found safety out on their own. So, he decided he too would run.

The man knew what awaited him if he was recaptured, the consequences would be worse than just being brought back to the plantation and beaten. He had seen what was done to others who had been returned after running. Still, he decided to take his chances and risk it all.

In the evening, as the dark of night set in, he slipped out of the cramped cabin, wary of waking his fellow captives and made his way across vast fields of the plantation unscathed. Weeks, then months, went by as he lived in hiding. Sometimes, only finding shelter under brush and wooded areas to sleep, he lived hour by hour just to survive.

He continued living this lifestyle for several years, until one day he was spotted by someone. When this stranger saw the man, he began to approach. The prospect of being recaptured was so overwhelming to the former slave that he fell into a fetal position and began to tremble knowing what lay ahead. However, to his surprise the stranger acted as if he meant no harm to the runaway. Instead, he leaned down, gently put his hand on the trembling man and asked, "Friend, why are you afraid?"

The runaway began to confess who he was and what he had been doing for these past years – hiding during the day and only sneaking out during the late hours to find food and water.

The men knelt together and as the runaway cried, the other man listened to his story. Once the story had been told and the tears subsided, the stranger placed his hand on the shoulder of the runaway and said, "But friend, haven't you heard? You're free!"

On that dreadful night when he fled the plantation in fear for his life, a very different thing was happening in the north. The Emancipation Proclamation had been enacted decreeing that all slaves in the

FIELD TIP:

The Emancipation Proclamation was effective January 1st, 1863. Most slaves in Texas were unaware of their freedom until June 19th, 1865. In 2021 "Juneteenth" became a federal holiday and is celebrated across the US.

Confederacy were to be set free. The runaway was gripped by fear the entire time he lived on the run simply because he did not know he was free.

I run into people every day who are ignorant of the truth about the Gospel. I shop at the same mall, eat at the same restaurants, and fly on the same airplanes as them. There are people who continue to live bound in their sin every day without ever knowing that someone has already come and set them free. They do not know that Jesus has paid the price for their sin. Our job as followers of Christ is to serve and love them enough to do the *unthinkable* and tell them about Jesus. Though we may struggle with fear and apprehension about sharing our faith, we must learn to overcome those fears for the sake of someone coming to know Jesus.

Romans 10:14 tells us that people will never know the truth about the gospel unless we tell them.[7] Matthew 28:19-20 says our responsibility as Christ followers is to make disciples.[8] So the time has come for us to leave our comfort zones, quit playing it safe, and begin doing the *unthinkable*. People will never know of the freedom that is found in Christ, unless we are the ones who step up and tell them.

NO MORE STAGE FRIGHT

In chapter two we discussed Matthew 16 and the story of Simon Peter. Simon was a follower of Jesus who had a lot of setbacks. We mentioned that in the original language, the name "Simon" actually means "swaying reed". It's this idea of a piece of grain blowing back and forth by the wind. It is unstable. It also has been translated as, "sand-like". Suppose you step out onto a sandy beach; you might have a difficult time finding sound footing. If you have been to the ocean, then you know that sand is not the best foundation. Your feet sink while standing in the sand, making a level posture almost impossible.

Jesus knew that Simon felt like he was standing on a beach, unable to find his footing, but the Messiah had plans for Simon. He did not want Simon Peter to carry around this label of, "Wishy Washy," so Jesus changed his friends' name.

He said, "No longer will you be called 'Simon' but from today on you will be Peter." That's a whole lot better when you figure out that Peter when translated means, "Petros" or "Rock", giving him a much firmer image than before.

As strong a name as Peter is, he still struggled with boldness and confidence. He was passionate and ambitious at the wrong times and timid or afraid in the moments he needed to be bold. At times, I think we all struggle with boldness in our faith, we have had scenarios play out in our lives and responded differently than we should have. I do not want to draw out Peter's less than incredible moments and dog him, but I do want you to see some things that happened in the span of just a few hours. These moments will show you the kind of work that God did in Peter's heart and life.

John 13 describes the evening meal directly before Jesus' betrayal. Simon Peter was there as Jesus explained that someone would soon betray Him. Peter was as floored as everyone else when Jesus identified that it was Judas who was going to do it.

Matthew 26 gives an account of what happened when Jesus went to the garden to pray later that evening. He took Peter, James, and John with him. When I was younger, I used to get upset that the disciples continued to fall asleep, and that Jesus had to wake them up several times throughout the night. He

TODAY THE MIRACLE HAPPENS TO YOU...

said, "Could you not watch with me one hour?" I didn't understand the toll this situation must have taken on them. Jesus had informed these men that His life was in danger. Not only was He going to be betrayed, but one of His disciples was responsible for it! They must have been emotionally and mentally exhausted. Over the years there have certainly been times in my walk with God where I have felt similarly. When I wanted nothing more than to be present, helpful in any way I could, my body and mind were depleted. I could not help but give into weariness due to the strain of my own emotional stress and physical exhaustion.

As Jesus sat up praying, and the disciples slept, it was only a matter of time until Judas arrived with the temple guards to arrest Jesus. For Peter, this injustice would not stand, the guards would not take Jesus. It was not going to go down without a fight. After all, Jesus did just call him "the rock"! Peter, thinking himself the hero, pulled out his sword and cut off the ear of the high priest's servant, a man named Malchus. In line with his nature, Peter had chosen poorly. It was not the time to fight. Jesus commanded Peter to put the sword away. Jesus knew that what was happening needed to happen and was meant to happen. Jesus knew that God had planned for him to die. Stinging from Jesus' rebuke, Peter must have been filled with confusion.

As Jesus was taken away by the group of soldiers and officials to be tried and later crucified, His disciples scattered. Many went into hiding. Simon Peter tried to follow Jesus without being noticed – but he fumbled that as well. On three separate occasions, just hours apart, Peter denied knowing Jesus. Falling into old habits, he was behaving more like Simon, than Peter, "the rock".

As events progressed, the disciples, Simon Peter included, were at a loss. The man they had given up everything to follow was dead, buried in a tomb. Jesus rose from the dead and His body was missing, but Peter did not know what to do next. As we read in John 20, Peter was out in his boat fishing with some other disciples when they saw a figure standing on the shore. The silhouette looked familiar, as he walked to the edge of the water.

"Have you caught anything," the figure from the shore called. "No," the men replied, though they had cast their nets all day and night, they had nothing to show for it.

Again, the man called out, saying, "Throw your net on the other side of the boat."

So, over the side their nets flew and so large was the catch that they were unable to haul the net into the boat.

Peter, realizing the figure on land was Jesus, dove into the water and made his way to shore. Jesus had come to meet with him and their conversation over breakfast changed everything.

Later in Acts 1 and 2, we see a drastic transformation in Peter from a man lacking confidence to "the rock" matching his new name. He no longer had any stage fright! It was Peter who stood before a crowd of thousands of people on the day of Pentecost when more than three thousand gave their

...SO TOMORROW THE MIRACLE CAN HAPPEN THROUGH YOU!

lives to Jesus.

Why? What happened to Simon Peter? What did Jesus say to him? Jesus told Peter the same thing He asks of us today - that we fulfill God's vision for the world and share our experience of Jesus' love with all humanity. If we love Jesus, we will share His message and take care of His children. Here's the good news, God has a plan and a purpose for your life, and He will equip you for it.

Waiting on the Lord, 120 people met together for prayer, honoring some of Jesus' last directions while here on Earth. In what would become known as the Day of Pentecost, those waiting in the upper room were filled with the Holy Spirit and they were empowered to change the world. The fact that you and I know the name of Jesus and continue to study His word is a testimony to those who obeyed his final commands. God gave them a boldness unlike any they had before. In the same way, you and I can experience boldness and empowerment from the Holy Spirit to accomplish the mission He's given us to finish.

Some have this idea that the empowerment of the Holy Spirit was only for the early New Testament church. However, in Acts 2:38-42, Peter clearly tells us this gift is for us and our children today. Sharing your faith is intimidating at times, and you may feel you lack the boldness to speak. I sometimes do as well, but we can't let fear rule us. Trust God to give you the tools to share your faith and do not miss out on the opportunities God places in your life each day.

You might be thinking, why do we need the Holy Spirit? What does He do for us in our daily walk? Think of Him as a guide, His gentle nudges give us insight into God's plan for our lives. The Holy Spirit is just as much a part of our daily lives as Jesus himself is. The Spirit of the Lord is mentioned over

90 times throughout the Old and New Testaments. The book of John gives insight into the purpose of the Holy Spirit, also called the Helper or the Comforter. Not only does He reveal scripture, but He also strengthens and uplifts us.

God never changes. He is outside of time, all knowing, and His words are true. His mercy is unfailing, but how wonderful is it that He gives us the Holy Spirit to help us daily?

I know it's cliché, but I am an Apple Acolyte. No disrespect to my Microsoft friends, Apple is simply the company I have leaned into the most over the past 15 years. Today, I have an iPhone, Apple Watch, and a MacBook that I use daily. I think the way that Apple seamlessly configures all their products to work together is magnificent. I use the interconnectivity constantly and it makes my life easier.

It seems like every few weeks there is a new iOS update, available for download and geared towards keeping everything in sync. Updating with each patch helps my devices work better and keeps them safe from being compromised by outsiders! That is who the Holy Spirit is for us. Serving as a constant source of strength, empowerment, and protection for our lives. But living without His help and guidance is like functioning on an outdated operating system. Without Him, you are vulnerable, operating below peak ability, and you are not using all the tools you have been given by God. Having access to the Holy Spirit is like having a fresh download available to you every day.

However, if we want to do the **unthinkable**, and serve others, then we need to invite the Holy Spirit into our lives to reveal God's plan for us each day. Remember, there are lives hanging in the balance and it is our prime directive to serve others and do whatever is necessary to get them to Jesus!

FIELD NOTES

KEY IDEAS:

- Saved people serve people!
- It is up to us to do whatever it takes to get people to Jesus.
- The message of the Gospel that we bring is so important that we must be willing to share it, even when doing so means looking ridiculous to the people around us.

FOLLOW-UP QUESTIONS:

1. What is your greatest fear about sharing your faith?
2. Who might God be speaking to you about right now?
3. Have you ever asked God to empower you to be a bolder witness for Him?

FIELD
NOTES

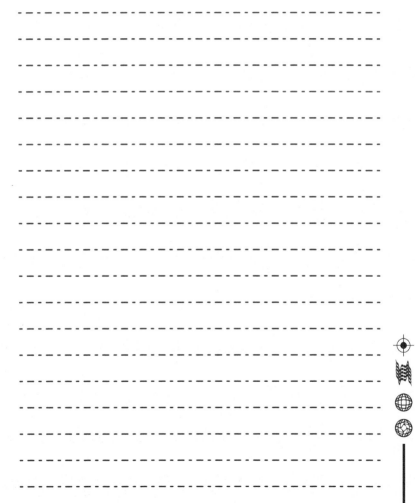

CHAPTER SEVEN · CHAPTER SEVEN · CHAPTER SEVEN · CHAPTER SEVEN · CHAPTER SEVEN · CHAPTER SEVEN ·

PERSEVERE FEARLESSLY

[8]"What is more, I consider everything a loss because of the surpassing worth of knowing Christ Jesus my Lord, for whose sake I have lost all things. I consider them garbage, that I may gain Christ [9]and be found in Him, not having a righteousness of my own that comes from the law, but that which is through faith in Christ—the righteousness that comes from God on the basis of faith."

Philippians 3:8-9

NO REGRETS

In 1904, William Borden, who was the heir to the Borden Dairy Estate, graduated from high school in Chicago. At barely 18, he was already a millionaire. A million dollars then would equal over 30 million today, which would make him a multimillionaire by our standards. His family decided that as a graduation gift they were going to send him on a trip around the world. The itinerary would take him from Asia to the Middle East and all throughout Europe. During those trips, after experiencing a stark contrast to the wealth and privilege he had been born into, William Borden grew to have a heart for people. So, still on his trip, he wrote home telling his family he planned to train for the ministry.

William decided to devote his life to ministry, and at that point in time in the back of his Bible, he wrote these words, "No Reserves". Borden resolved to hold nothing back. He traveled home, and after furthering his education, graduated from Yale University at the top of his class. After graduation, he again wrote in his Bible, just under "No Reserves" he wrote the words, "No Retreats". William, knowing that his wealth and education would afford him any number of choices in life, he wanted to leave himself no room for retreats from his chosen path. He told himself that he was going to do what God called him to, no matter what.

Shortly thereafter, he went to training in Cairo, Egypt. Though he felt called to the mission field in China, he stopped in Egypt to train and prepare himself for the work ahead. After just one month in Egypt, William contracted cerebral meningitis and passed away a month later.

William never made it to China to the mission field where he was headed. Some might say he failed, that his was a life wasted, barely lived. They might lament that with his immense fortune and intellect, he could have done so much more, been so much better, lived an extraordinary life. His own family might have wished they never gave him that graduation gift a few years earlier.

A few months later, after receiving his belongings in the mail, William's family was sorting through the last of his possessions. As his family was looking through his Bible, they leafed to the back and there, saw the words he had written. "No Reserves." "No Retreats". Below those, as if just recently penned, were two new words. They realized he must have written them in the final months or even weeks of his life. William's final note to himself, his final message to remember was, "No Regrets".[1]

You see, William was called by God, he knew that whatever came of his life, he could move forward without reservations, retreats, or regrets, because his steps were directed by God. In the same way, God is calling us to persevere and to live a life of no regrets! Regardless if the rest of the world views our choices like we are wasting our time, our money, our education and even our very lives, we do not belong to the world, it has nothing for us. We are linked to a higher calling, a greater purpose. However, the most important thing we can do is to live our lives with no regrets.

The question that God has been asking me quite a bit lately is, "Am I willing to look stupid for Him?" As a teenager, it was my constant worry that my friends would view my faith and think I was weird because of it.

As I wrote this book, a man in my 40's, I still struggle with some of those same thoughts. Lately, God has been asking me which is more important – having a radically passionate and **unthinkable** faith or being accepted by others?

As followers of God desiring to do the **unthinkable** with our lives, we need to be willing to live out our faith with passion unlike anything the world has ever seen. As John Wesley said, "Light yourself on fire with passion and people will come for miles to watch you burn."[2] The time is now to stop worrying about what others think and like Paul, count everything else as loss for the sake of Jesus being glorified. I want to challenge you today to live like William Borden...

NO RESERVES
NO RETREATS
NO REGRETS!

MIDDLE OF THE ROCK

There is a mountain that is popular among hiking enthusiasts and more casual climbers alike. It has wonderful views as you ascend and while the ascent is quite difficult, the view from the peak is spectacular. For those who choose to climb it, the journey is possible, if the climbers stay focused and persevere. Those who have climbed the mountain describe the journey this way.

Climbers set out on the trek to the top of the mountain totally energized and ready to go. Spirits are high and expectations are great. However, about a quarter of the way up the mountain some of the challenges of the climb begin to set in. The altitude makes the air difficult to breathe, the energy spent already begins to create an intense hunger, while the cold temperatures of the mountain cause hands and feet to tingle and begin going numb. Halfway up the mountain a lodge was built where people can check-up and rest, catch a bite to eat, and get a quick warm up by the fire. It's a neat place indeed. From the comfort of the lodge, out an expansive picture window, weary travelers can gaze at the top and watch climbers who are passing by, continuing toward the peak.

After hearing about this amazing location, something was told to me that I found quite staggering. According to a study taken at this particular lodge, over two-thirds who set foot inside the building never go on to see the top of the mountain. For most of them, the lodge becomes the end of the road. Why? It happens when people stay in the comfort of the structure for too long and become comfortable, too comfortable to continue. The cozy lodge, with its soft furnishings, blazing fire and other amenities cause most travelers to take their focus off their initial purpose and lose sight of their chosen goal.

The word *mediocre* is literally translated from Latin as "halfway up the mountain".[3] No one wants to be called mediocre, and no one who sets out to get to the top of a mountain should be content with stopping half-way up. When we listen to the words of Paul in Philippians 3:12-14 we can feel empowered in our daily lives. He says,

> *"Not that I have already obtained this or am already perfect, but I press on to make it my own, because Christ Jesus has made me His own. Brothers, I do not consider that I have made it my own. But one thing I do: Forgetting what is behind and straining toward what is ahead, I press on toward the goal to win the prize for which God has called me heavenward in Christ Jesus."[4]*

At times, life is tough, and we can find ourselves in circumstances and situations that are tiring, draining, or even painful. There are seasons that can be so taxing, we feel worn thin. The world will look at our struggle and find the perseverance of our continued efforts in the face of exhaustion **unthinkable**. When we as Christian's experience trouble, or trials, like the world does, and yet we refuse to give up, it displays our reliance on God. When we do not allow our situations to diminish the works of God in our lives, we bring him glory, and show his power to others.

Choosing to follow Jesus will not make life easy. Work is still work. Disappointment and frustration are still real. Taxes are still inevitable, and death still hits too close to home. Yet the world is watching with eyes-wide open, and how we navigate through these difficult seasons serves as a testimony for God to unbelievers that will make their jaws drop. Yes, we still face hopeless situations, but because of Jesus we are not without hope!

KILIMANJARO: SUMMIT DAY
FRIDAY, SEPTEMBER 20TH, 2013

We woke up at 4:30 am for tea and bread in bed. We did that to stay warm. We stepped out of our tents with our headlamps on and departed sharply at 5 am. This time we did not pack. We would be needing to crash for a bit after coming back from the summit.

Our first challenge came when we had to climb over an icy rock formation. It was heart pounding and scary, but we made it. We then continued on in the darkness.

Eventually the sun crested and began to show itself. Uhuru peak was getting bigger, and its snowy glaciers were more visible than ever. At first, we moved through red rock. Then the floor became pebbly and harder to grip. We found ourselves zigging and zagging - doing switchbacks all the way up. Like Hobbits heading to the top of Mordor!

The entire time we were acclimating perfectly, but we were becoming physically exhausted. It was one-step forward and a half a slide back.

We reached Stella Point at 10:30 am and continued on. Finally, at 11:03 am, what we had come to do we had accomplished. We had reached Uhuru peak, the tallest point in Africa.

I have to admit that it was a little emotional turning the corner and seeing that big green sign!

After a short time of pictures and taking in the sights we proceeded down and back to camp. Yes, we had accomplished something huge, but who cares if you never live to brag about it. It was time to head home.

BE CAREFUL WHAT YOU WISH FOR

After sharing with you our journey of finding a permanent location and renovating for our campus in Bricktown, I can say without any reservation that it was among the top three hardest things that I have ever done in my life. I know that many of my friends and family at Newhope Church feel the same way. You have probably heard the saying, "Be careful what you wish for because you just might get it all." For me the summer of 2017 proved this saying true when demo on our new space began. When we purchased the old comedy club on Sheridan Avenue, we had just celebrated our second birthday. I think I can speak for most church planters when I say that the struggle to have a permanent location is real. The weekly grind of setting up and tearing down for services can feel cumbersome and at times thankless. This feeling came even though we were on the fast track. Most new churches will live a somewhat nomadic lifestyle, being portable for at least seven years. We knew we were blessed.

We made our purchase and began the process of demolition and submitting plans to the city. I knew that pastoring a church without a permanent location was tough, requiring hours of set up and tear down each week, but I never imagined the extra weight and work that would be involved when throwing renovations into the mix. As a cost cutting measure, I also took on the responsibility of steering the project as a general contractor – something that Bible College had never prepared me for. As a church family, we went to work, and we labored hard for the cause. I slept no more than five hours a night for the next ten months, working at all hours to achieve the dream God had given me for our church.

My life was operating at an unprecedented level. I was completely uncomfortable, being stretched and challenged in ways I never imagined, and it was one of the best times of my life. Of course, it was hard, every step of the way, but I knew perseverance gave way for hope and if I moved forward fearlessly, we would end with an incredible place to meet as a church. In addition, I would encounter personal spiritual growth as well.

When you are walking through trials, like those mentioned in James 1, it is certainly not fun, but the truth feels palpable when he says, "Consider it pure joy, my brothers and sisters, whenever you face trials of many kinds, because you know that the testing of your faith produces perseverance."[5]

Be careful then in what you wish for because you just might get it all. You might find yourself walking through a tough season, but if you persevere, God will birth something in you that might have never happened otherwise.

FAIL FORWARD

One reason people give up and do not press in is because they are afraid to fail. Fear is a terrible excuse because unless you quit, failure is never final. The only problem with failure comes when we quit before we have finished. Failure has wounded leaders and caused them to limp off alone to lick their wounds, like a wild animal in a nature documentary. That urge to withdraw is dangerous and it is exactly what the enemy of God wants us to do in our exasperated moment of failure.

After all, 1 Peter 5:8 tells us that, "our enemy the devil is like a roaring lion."[6] He wants to defeat us. On our own, we are no match for him, but when we stay in our pack, we can face our enemy together. To avoid falling prey to the enemy and allowing failure to make us feel like failures, we must fail forward and learn from our missed moments.

Failure is perhaps life's greatest teacher. It was Thomas Alva Edison who invented the light bulb. However, it took him more than 10,000 attempts before he was able to make a successful working prototype. Someone once asked Edison, how did he handle failing all those thousands of times? How did he find the courage to keep going? Edison replied, "I have not failed 10,000 times. I have not failed once. I have succeeded in proving that those 10,000 ways will not work."[7] Suppose we lived in a world where we all had that perspective, that is what perseverance looks like.

Every week in our staff meeting we not only celebrate the wins at our church, but we openly discuss our failures, mistakes, and the things that we could improve on. Every person on the team owns both the mission and the mistakes, and we are all determined and committed to make it better together. I am a believer that if you are not making mistakes then you are not taking big enough risks. You are playing it too safe! We cannot let our fear of failure rob us of God's blessings or deter us from His path. Do not be afraid to fail, be afraid of not trying hard enough.

It was also Thomas Edison who said, "Many of life's failures are people who did not realize how close they were to success when they gave up."[8] So often, people quit right before their breakthrough is about to happen. Instead, dig your heels in, stand your ground and fight a little bit longer. Do not give up but press in and as you grit your teeth and brace for impact, watch what God does through your determination and strength.

TRAINING WITH THE RIGHT PEOPLE

Proverbs 13:20 says, "Walk with the wise and become wise for a companion of fools suffers harm."[9] One of the biggest challenges to living a life that is **unthinkable** is learning who to do life with and who to have on the journey beside you. The people we surround ourselves with each day are who will fuel us, they will either make us sharper, better tools for God's use, or wear us down, making our edges blunt and rendering us dull, and useless.

The day I committed to climb Kilimanjaro, I began to look for people who had an interest in going so that I could have someone to train with. Training is never easy, but it is more tolerable when you have someone by your side working toward the same goal. It is why we have gym buddies, accountability partners, sponsors, personal trainers, life coaches, and tutors. However, not everyone who wants to do life with you will have the same goals that you do. As a student pastor, I broke down into three categories the kinds of people who might try to join you on your life journey.

The first group I called, *Pullers*. These are people who for whatever reason, are not walking side-by-side with you spiritually. They are what Paul would have meant when he said in 2 Corinthians 6 to not be "unequally yoked".[10] These are not inherently bad people, but they are not interested in going where you are going. Often, the weight of their agenda, goals, and opinions can weigh us down. They are always behind you trying to catch up. They reach for you, grab at you and sometimes it is inadvertent, but regardless they slow you down and drag you backwards.

The second group of people are *Putters*. They are people who sit shotgun in your car and do life with you. They putt around town with you. These people are fun, they can bring you joy and fill your cup. You are after the same things in your walk with God, and because you are going to the same place, they can keep in step with you. They may not offer much growth potential to give you, but at the same time they are not going to pull you backwards. These people are running beside you.

There is a third group of people, I call them *Pushers*. These people are at the place with God in their lives that you wish you were. Pushers mentor you and speak wisdom over your life. Providing you with ideas and influencing you towards good things, Pushers, the opposite of Pullers, propel you forward. They are literally like wind at your back pushing you along your chosen path.

Do not misunderstand me here. We have a place for all three of these kinds of people in our lives. After all, without pullers tugging at us, who are we going to share Jesus with? I would classify the prostitutes and the tax collectors that Jesus spent time ministering to as pullers. I think if Jesus has them, so too should we. However, when it comes to persevering, it is imperative that we surround ourselves with people who are on the same mission we are.

We all find it difficult to train for things by ourselves, but if we surround ourselves with people who are at odds with us, suddenly the difficulty increases. A friend once told me upon seeing a 26.2-mile decal on the back window of my car that he could probably consume that number of Oreos in one sitting. As I write this portion of the book, I am currently in training for marathon number two, and guess who is not helping me with that training? When we allocate our time, we need to look to people who have been where we want to go and done the work needed to get there. If we work alongside people who have the same goals, we will be better equipped to achieve our own.

The writer of Proverbs 17:7 reminds us that, "As iron sharpens iron, so one man sharpens another."[11] This verse is not saying that allowing ourselves to be sharpened is an easy task. It does not say we will enjoy the process or that everyone on our same journey will tell us nice things we want to hear. It promises us that if we seek out others with our same iron will, determination and motivation to push us to succeed in God's plan, they will cause us to be better. I happen to think that when iron rubs up against iron it probably produces friction and some sparks, but some friction can be to our benefit if we are going to see results in the end.

So, if our aim is to persevere fearlessly and catch the gaze of the world, then we need each other. There is only one person who has ever done anything amazing on His own. His name is Jesus. He was the Son of God, a sinless and perfect man, but even He had disciples to do life with. Let us look to His example and allow others in our lives who will walk with us to help push us forward.

FIELD NOTES

KEY IDEAS:

- May our motto be that of William Borden who said, "No Reserves, No Retreats, No Regrets."
- Failure is not fatal if failure is not final. Learn from your failure and let it propel you forward.
- If we catch on fire, people will come for miles to watch us burn.

FOLLOW-UP QUESTIONS:

1. Who are the people in my life that are potential pullers that could hold me back?
2. Who are the people in my life who are putters and are on a similar journey that I am on?
3. Who are the people in my life who are pushers? Of those, who are my mentors? Do I need to find more?

FIELD NOTES

PART THREE

WRITTEN IN THE **DNA** OF EVERY PERSON

IS A DESIRE TO ACHIEVE **GREATNESS**

TO MAKE THEIR **MARK**

AND TO LEAVE A **LEGACY.**

Simon Sinek, a motivational speaker popular in the business world wrote an inspiring book entitled, *Start With Why*. Well Simon, I apologize for not starting this book with "why", but I do plan to end there.

In chapters one through three, I introduced "what" this idea of **unthinkable** living is. We dove deeper in talking about *doing the hard things*, *the underdog mindset*, and *getting to the spot*.

We just concluded part two and spent time explaining "how" to live an **unthinkable** life. Things like *forgiving easily*, *giving generously*, *serving sacrificially*, and *persevering fearlessly* are not simply obtainable, but are an essential to the Christian life God has called everyone to live.

That leads us to the third and final part of this book where we take a few minutes to answer the burning question: "Why?"

Now, I must admit that this part has me excited! When we put into practice what God desires of us – what I have been discussing throughout this book – it is going to produce fruit in your life.

My hope for you is as you near the end of this book you will be inspired to live your life intentionally. When that happens, the people in your life will take notice and be drawn to our incredible, loving God.

WANT TO KNOW HOW MUCH IMPACT THIS PLAN CAN HAVE ON YOUR LIFE? READ ON!

CHAPTER EIGHT · CHAPTER EIGHT · CHAPTER EIGHT · CHAPTER EIGHT · CHAPTER EIGHT · CHAPTER EIGHT · CHAPTER EIGHT · CHAPTER EIGHT ·

LEAVE YOUR MARK

²"You yourselves are our letter, written on our hearts, known and read by everyone."

2 Corinthians 3:2

THE BIG PICTURE

As a lover of podcasts, I found one that as an entrepreneur, I absolutely love. Produced by NPR, the segment is called, *"How I Built This"* hosted by Guy Raz.

In one episode, Guy has a dialogue with Gary Erickson, the owner and founder of the Clif Bar.

Raz and Erickson banter back and forth, peppering the interview with little-known facts about the genesis of the company. In the years leading up to founding Clif Bar, Gary ran a bakery and in his free time had a passion for the outdoors. When I heard that Erickson was an avid distance cyclist, my interest was piqued, and I found myself enthused to hear where the interview was going.

Gary went on to explain that one day, while on a 175-mile ride, he found himself choking down yet another energy bar, when he said to himself, "I don't think I could eat another one of these nasty things." It was then, mid chew as the lackluster flavor of stale ingredients and bargain bin energy bits crossed his taste buds, that it hit him. He owned his shop, what was stopping him from making his own energy bar? He knew flavor pairings that could make a bar taste good, and his high-quality ingredients would provide the nutrients that bikers, hikers, and climbers would need. That is how it all started. Out of exasperation at the problem of what bars were available, followed by the ingenuity to solve the problem.

So, he created the Clif Bar, named to honor his father–Clifford. Several years after founding the company, it had become a grand success. His idea, and his products were now worth several million dollars. My favorite part of the entire discussion came as Erickson described a pivotal moment in his company. He continued, "We employed thousands of people and I took pride in the fact that our company could provide jobs and take care of families."

At that time, someone approached Gary and his business partner and offered to buy the company for a sizably generous amount. A tentative agreement was reached for the lucrative deal. But only hours before signing the paperwork Gary concluded he just could not go through with it.

When asked why, he casually replied, "I realized that if I sold this company, I'd literally be giving away my legacy. After all, the Clif Bar was named after my dad. I just couldn't do it."[1]

What a powerful story, but what does any of that have to do with living an **unthinkable** life? We already know that what Gary did might seem **unthinkable** to some, but what I want to point out is why he did it. No matter what, he did not want to lose his legacy, and we can apply that same principle to our lives. We cannot lose sight of the legacy we have been called to leave. Our legacy means so much more than just what this life has to offer. We are called to a higher purpose, to God's glorious purpose. Keeping that legacy in mind will help us to not give up even if we are faced with the choice of an easier path.

When thinking about our legacy, I cannot help but remember in 2018, as we were preparing to relocate into our newly renovated space in Bricktown. We had a special night of prayer with our families just before we laid flooring in our auditorium. Amongst people worshiping together, writing prayers on exposed studs and plywood, I witnessed the importance of legacy.

I watched Eric and Melinda Allison and their five girls pray together. Having just written down their prayers and dreams, they were wrapped in dad's arms and praying together. That picture, the weight of it, that family and their future, it reminded me once again that the stakes were high.

I continued reading the plywood boards and unpainted sheetrock and saw where someone else had written a prayer for the future children of The Bridge who had not yet been born. That prayer, the idea of building a community of believers, that is what leaving a legacy is all about!

Just as Gary Erickson with the Clif Bar company, we cannot afford to let our legacy be sold to the highest bidder. We must live in God's *unthinkable* plan and purpose for our lives. Our legacy is not for sale. Each of us is a part of the Body of Christ, an integral member who has a destiny and is building a legacy to leave, and how we leave it is up to us. Entire generations of people have lived their lives without thinking about their choices, and how they were affecting those closest to them. Take the Israelites. The choices of a few caused 40 years of wandering in the desert instead of living in the Promised Land, simply because they lacked faith to live in the **unthinkable** places. Let us not make the same error.

A friend of mine, John Van Pay, pastors Gateway Fellowship Church in San Antonio, Texas. John also climbed Kilimanjaro several years ago. John recently wrote a book titled, *Marathon Faith*. One day while having lunch, John told me a story that is in the book. He said his porter, a man by the name of Jamaica, asked him what his goal was. John said emphatically, "To make it to the top of the mountain!"

Surprisingly, Jamaica shook his head in disappointment, "No, John," he said. "It's not to get to the top of the mountain, but it's to make it back home safely to your family."

Sometimes I think we miss it, the big picture I mean. We hustle, we keep our heads down, we work as hard as we can, but for all the wrong reasons. We treat life like some giant cosmic scoreboard, as if the goals are measured in earthly possessions or accolades. The *"lived their best life"* trophy goes to the person with the highest position, the fullest schedule, the nicest home, or the biggest bank account. All that work so we can leave everything we own to our family as an inheritance. In the end though, life is not a game. Regardless of what you leave behind, if there was a cosmic scoreboard, God would be looking to our actions, our intentions, and motivations to show how to assign points. Thankfully, God does not treat our humanity as some kind of game. He created us, He loves us, and He wants our goal to be living our lives to please Him, focusing on growing close to Him and sharing our faith. When our time on earth does end, the journey will have been about getting to Jesus, going to heaven, and taking as many people with us as we can.

With a career in ministry spanning more than 20 years, we are privileged to have worked alongside some of the best children's pastors. We spent 14 of those years in student ministry ourselves. In both children's and youth ministries, you might think the goal is to train up kids who love Jesus, but that is only half of what we are trying to accomplish. More than training children, we want to raise them up into adults who are just as passionately in love with Jesus as they were as children. What scares me is that we will not know if we were successful for many years to come. We want Jesus to be the first love of every single young adult that grew up in our ministry. That is what it means to see the big picture, and I truly believe that we are on the right track.

MOMENTS OF SIGNIFICANCE

Not long ago, I came across the term, *epoch*. It shares its pronunciation with the more familiar word, "epic" however its meaning is vastly different. An *epoch* is defined as the beginning of a period marked by a significant event, this can be either in the life of a person, or within the world timeline.[2] Regardless, an epoch becomes a point of reference for historians and is regarded as a highly significant point on the timeline. Everything from the inception of that epoch on, is either referenced as having taken place before it or after.

As I thought about the definition of an epoch, I tried to list a few events that would qualify – the most recent being the worldwide pandemic caused by Covid-19 and the most obvious being the life, death, and resurrection of Jesus Christ. His coming was so significant that today our dates use the labels BC and AD to denote the years in the Gregorian or

Julian calendars. BC means *"before Christ"* and AD originates from the Latin, *"anno domini nostril Jesu Christi"*. Roughly translated this means, "in the year of our Lord" for a simple reason. Our Lord is still alive. His actions thousands of years ago are still changing hearts and lives today.

In thinking of Jesus, my mind turned to the events in the Bible leading up to and foreshadowing His coming. Scriptures tell of other auspicious beginnings. Like the day that Moses parted the Red Sea or when Joshua prayed for the sun to stand still. And even the day that the veil in the temple was torn in two, doing away with the old law and the old sacrificial system.

There have been countless moments in history of great magnitude. Many have been lost to the annuls of time, while others are still affecting our lives today. We should hold onto the thought that every day we could impact someone's life. By living out the **unthinkable** daily we can help them do something momentously significant. We can speak into the lives of those around us and use our influence to lead them to Christ – to change their path into eternity. This is a chance to help them create an epochal moment in their lives. An epic epoch!

The saying goes that the two greatest days in your life are the day you were born and the day that you realized why.[3] As followers of Christ, we have the opportunity to help reveal the purpose God placed in each of our lives. We can share the truth with those around us and help them find God's purpose for their own lives.

Rarely are people remembered for ordinary choices. Sometimes it can feel like our everyday lives are filled with moments that will be forgotten, that have no impact on eternity. Only the extraordinary things that create epochal moments are captured and passed onto future generations. The catch to all of this is God determines which of our ordinary choices will become extraordinary. With God, the mundane done faithfully can become the miraculous. The humdrum of everyday can become a symphony. God sees the whole story of humanity. He alone knows which choices will lead to astonishing change. Our responsibility is faithfulness.

So, listen for His voice. Be attentive to the subtle nudges from the Holy Spirit and determine that you are going to use your life and influence to be a facilitator of epoch moments for other people.

CARVE CAREFULLY

Several years ago, construction workers were laying a foundation for a building outside the city of Pompeii. As they were digging, they uncovered the corpse of a woman who must have been fleeing from the eruption of Mt. Vesuvius but was caught in the rain of hot ashes. The architects noticed that the woman's hands clutched jewels, which were preserved in excellent condition. She had the jewels, but death had stolen it all.[4]

As I read that story, my heart broke because I thought of how often people die much like this woman - holding onto valuable truth and unable to pass it on. How often do people remain silent instead of sharing the good news of the Gospel that changes lives? Instead, I want to leave a legacy with my life. When my time on Earth comes to a close, I want to leave having been completely poured out into the lives of others.

Years ago, several missionaries, including Jim Elliot, moved to the jungles of Ecuador to reach the Quechua natives, hoping to share the Gospel with them. There was another tribe of indigenous people, the Huaorani, located farther into the wilderness than the missionaries had previously been, but Elliot wanted to try. After months of preparation, fly overs with their pilot Nate Saint, and brief exchanges with Huaorani natives, Jim along with Nate and a few others built a base a short distance from the Huaorani village, along the Curaray River. Their plans to share the Gospel and meet with the tribe were cut short when warriors from the tribe surrounded and killed them. Jim's words written in his journal, recovered after his death should remind us to leave our mark, to persevere. He wrote, "He is no fool who gives what he cannot keep to gain that which he cannot lose."[5]

Written in the DNA of every person is a desire to achieve greatness, to make their mark, and to leave a legacy. While greatness may look different for each person, I doubt that having a large bank account, the nicest home, or being number one in the company is really what any of us hides in the deepest desires of our hearts. The *unthinkable* way to make your mark is through affecting the lives of people. I love what Charles Spurgeon, a famed English Baptist preacher says, "Carve your name on hearts and not on marble."[6] In other words, our goal should be to love others. It is about the way that we impact lives, not history.

Paul, in 2 Corinthians 3:2 writes, "You yourselves are our letter, written on our hearts, known and read by everyone."[7] He is telling the people that their lives are a testament to the work that has been completed, they are his living legacy. We need to remember that we have a set number of hours to impact the lives of others on earth, so let us not waste them. Let your focus be on the time you spend loving and investing in people, not trying to obtain money, possessions, or popularity. Focus on God's real currency – His children.

HOBBY LEGACY

A few years ago, on a Wednesday night in Oklahoma City, I had the privilege of hearing Max Lucado speak. Max is a prominent evangelical pastor at Oak Hills Church in San Antonio, Texas. He shared with the audience that while doing a book signing that day, he had been invited to tour the corporate offices of Hobby Lobby, Mardel, and Hemispheres Furniture. During his time there, he was also able to participate in their corporate board meeting.

Max told us just how impressed he was with the company and their warehouses with 20 miles of conveyor belts, but then he leaned into the audience and his voice changed. It was almost as if he was about to share something with the rest of us that might get him in trouble. He went on to say, "but something that impressed me the most was what happened after the board meeting."

He said, "After all of the executives and leaders left the room, the rest of the Green family," (the Green family are the founders and current owners of the company), "entered the room and took their seats at the board room table." He made sure to emphasize that it was the entire family, including all the children and the grandchildren.

FIELD TIP:

Hobby Lobby started as a small business in the Green family's garage. Today there are more than 900 stores, and over 43,000 employees nationwide.

Max went on to describe what he saw with a smile on his face, as he said, "And for the next several hours they opened letters, and they read them, they prayed together, and then they decided collectively what projects they were going to take on, where they were going to send their money and who their company was going to bless."

I once heard Robert Morris, the pastor of Gateway Church in Dallas, Texas explain his view on the progression of parenting. We first *teach* a child because they are too young to know themselves. So, we must first show them. When they grow older, we then *train* them. They no longer need us to show them, but we are right there beside them helping as they grow and learn to do it on their own. We employ those two steps so that we can then *trust* them when they are older to make the right decisions when we are not around.[8]

Now, I think this works with almost anything you are helping your children with as they grow up, but I especially think it's true with this idea of leaving a legacy.

You see, the Green family could have easily let the grown-ups make all the "grown-up" decisions. The work could have been something that one or two of the family members oversaw. However, for David Green and his family, this was more than about giving out financial assistance. They treated it as an opportunity to teach their children and their grandchildren about giving, loving others, and leaving a legacy!

When it comes to my children, Kierstyn and Ryan and the people we are ministering to, Kate and I want to be intentional with the calling God has placed on our lives. We want to pass on the mission and calling so the legacy we leave will outlast us, propelling generations to come.

SETBACKS

In life, setbacks are inevitable, and disappointments are unavoidable. No one really wants to talk about them and honestly, I did not want to write about them. My goal though, is to help you live out the **unthinkable** in your walk with God, and I would not be giving you the whole picture if I avoided the hard parts. Jesus reminded us in the gospels that, "In this life you will have trouble."[9] Our troubles tend to come on the heels of seasons where we have put in hard work, creeping in to hamstring us just as we are busting our tails for the Lord.

While training for my first marathon at the age of 30, I worked hard to prepare, and my body responded. I was experiencing back pain. Thinking this pain was common, a result of running 20 to 30 miles a week, I tried to soak it away in a hot bath, using heat pads, but nothing seemed to do the trick. I just could not seem to shake it. I gave in and went to see our family physician. As I sat in her office and described my pain, she began to look at my back and sides. After a few moments, she asked me, "How long have you had those spots on your side?" She pointed to a small rash where my shirt had rubbed my skin raw. When you run for long distances, this rug-burn-like rash is not uncommon. I pointed to my side, and she said, "Yep, those spots. How long have they been there?" I told her that they had developed over the last couple of days.

FAILURE IS NOT FINAL UNLESS WE ALLOW IT TO BE

She responded, "I know you're young and it's not very common, but I'm pretty sure you have put your body under so much stress that you have shingles."

I wish I could tell you that she gave me a quick prescription and I was right back at it but having shingles really set me back. Right in the middle of training the doctor ordered me to back off for two weeks. I had to postpone some of my bigger runs, it really was a challenge. Something was happening to me during those two weeks, though. It was during this time of healing where I learned that setbacks are setups for big comebacks. After a few weeks off I put my head down, continued my training, and completed my marathon as planned.

Life can be like that, filled with unexpected starts and stops, but if we continue to be faithful, God can show up and use our challenges for His glory.

A friend of mine who planted a church several years ago, his team was filled with friends. He ended up having to part ways with his best friend and another member of his team had a spouse who was unfaithful. Those proved to be difficult times, and immense setbacks but God remained faithful. There have been church plants who were still setting up and tearing down every week who have had their trailers full of equipment stolen. The fire marshal of the town told a local church on a Friday that their weekly meeting location, a theater they rented, was unsafe and until the owner got the building up to code, they had to cease meeting there. These situations are very real setbacks. There are multitudes of different setbacks we will face in our lifetime. Though we have not even scraped the surface of possible setbacks, it has never been about them, it's about how we respond to them that matters. Will we allow difficult challenges to pull us from the path that God has for us, or will we remain strong and courageous, persevering for Christ through our setbacks and into His glorious purpose for our lives?

It is not about how you fall, but how quickly you can get back up and continue. We shouldn't grovel in our setbacks because, through God, they can become the greatest teacher and motivator if we allow them. Failure is not final unless we allow it to be.

When our cause is worth living for, we must assume that there is an enemy seeking to hold us back and stop us short of making a difference with our lives.

We have come full circle, back to the story of Zacchaeus. Here was a man who could have looked at the circumstances of his life and chosen to quit. He persevered and as he climbed the tree to see Jesus, his life was forever changed, and a legacy formed. More than 2,000 years later, we are still reading his story, still being inspired by his example and I can scarcely imagine the number of people in heaven today as a result of his *unthinkable* actions. His story is not done inspiring believers. As God's people daily look to the Bible for guidance, Zac and his story can continue to encourage us all.

Perhaps you struggle to forgive easily or give generously. Maybe serving selflessly is proving more difficult than you anticipated or you wrestle daily with persevering fearlessly. Those whose lives are *unthinkable* to the world are determined to keep going. We know that our legacy is on the line. So, we must remember that His purpose is greater than ours and that this is His battle to win. Let's be determined to see God's plans come to fruition and follow His path for our lives. Regardless of the setbacks the world throws in our way, we are more than conquerors. So let us live determined to make a difference, determined to leave a mark on the lives of others in a way that is exponential.

FIELD
NOTES

KEY IDEAS:

- Few are remembered for something that is ordinary, but God makes the ordinary into the extraordinary.
- A man is not a fool to give up what he cannot keep in order to gain what he cannot lose.
- Setbacks are setups for big comebacks!

FOLLOW-UP QUESTIONS:

1. How do you want to be remembered?
2. What are you doing intentionally to leave a legacy with your life?
3. Of the ways to live an *unthinkable* life by forgiving, giving, serving, and persevering which are easiest for you? In which of those *unthinkable* areas do you need to be extra intentional?

FIELD
NOTES

LIVE
EXPONENTIALLY

Now to Him who is able to do immeasurably more than all we ask or imagine, according to His power that is at work in us, to Him be glory in the church and in Christ Jesus throughout all generations, for ever and ever! Amen.

Ephesians 3:20-21

MULTIPLICATION, NOT ADDITION

We serve a God who can do incredible things. Paul in his letter to the church in Ephesus says, God is able to do things in a manner so miraculous, so *unthinkably glorious* that we cannot measure it.

Pretend that you and I are enjoying a cup of coffee and talking about a new business strategy we plan to start together. Though I hold ownership of the business and assume all the risk, I value our close friendship and want you involved in this startup. Think of this as a "negotiation talk" about what your compensation is going to look like. I provide options so you can choose your compensation schedule:

> *Option #1:* You receive a base salary and add $2 to your paycheck every week thereafter.

> *Option #2:* You receive a base salary and add $2 the first week and multiply those dollars by two every week thereafter.

When faced with these options, which would you choose?

Let us take a look at what your first-year salary would look like with both options. If you chose option #1, by the end of the year, on week fifty-two, you will have only added $104 extra dollars to your paycheck. Whereas, option #2, using multiplication, would lead to a compensation plan at week 53 that is 9.0072 times ten to the fifteenth power, or 9,007,200.000,000,000 (which I had to look up to list in standard terms). As you can see, that would be an astronomical amount of money. If, like me, you need to see how that works, look at the dynamic multiplication below:

Week 1: 2 x 2 = 4
Week 2: 2 x 4 = 8
Week 3: 2 x 8 = 16
Week 4: 2 x 16 = 32
Week 5: 2 x 32 = 64
Week 10: 2 x 512 = 1,024
Week 20: 2 x 524,288 = 1,048,576
Week 30: 2 x 536,870,912 = 1.073742 x 10^9
Week 52: 2 x 4.5036 x 1015 = 9.0072 x 10^{15}

If this were a real scenario it would be an ideal business agreement for you and secondly, you would love me as a partner. My point is that multiplication is better.

When the principle of compound interest is at work, things begin to double, and that number grows exponentially. Just as you would elect to grow your money, I want to encourage you to choose to multiply your life by investing in others. I've heard it said that you can count the number of seeds in an apple, but you cannot count the number of apples in a seed. That seed will one day become a tree and then later, bear fruit. Year after year it will create more and more fruit with more and more seeds. Eventually, the tree will yield hundreds of thousands of apples. In those apples will be several seeds that when planted will produce even more trees full of apples. Sure, some of those apples will be eaten and their seeds will remain unused, but remember, all those apples are a result of one seed. In hardly any time at all, that single seed from one apple turns into 9.0072×10^{15} apples.

What do all these apples have to do with you or me? We can look to the Bible and the story of Abraham to show us what living exponentially looks like.

GOD'S PROMISE TO ABRAHAM

Having discussed this story in chapter five, we are viewing it here through a different lens. In Genesis 22, God told Abraham that he would have more children than he would be able to count. Does that sound familiar? God went on to promise that Abraham's family would be exponentially large, innumerable like the grains of sand on the earth. However, Abraham and Sarah were getting old and were, at this point, childless. Such a shock was this news to an aging Sarah that she laughed out loud.

Abraham and Sarah lived near the Negev, a vast desert near Egypt. Surrounded by sand, childless, and aging, consider how Sarah and Abraham might have been viewing God's promise. Essentially, God said to Abraham, "Look, see the sand surrounding you? I will make your descendants so numerous that they will outnumber the grains of sand in the desert".

On your next beach visit, or when you notice kids in a sandbox at play, I dare you to try and count the grains of sand, even in just one handful. While you could do it, the task is a grueling one, and nearly impossible to complete. God planned for the seed of Abraham to exponentially explode in size, and God always keeps his promises. Abraham's descendants are still around today in the modern world. The entirety of the modern Jewish nation today is a result of God's promise to Abraham.

EXPONENTIAL GROWTH

In 2017, on a Sunday in September, we helped welcome the third location of The Bridge Church in Piedmont, Oklahoma. In the small suburb of Oklahoma City was the fourth campus opened with Jason and Shara Taylor as the lead pastors. We partnered with our parent location, who also helped to launch our campus, through prayer, fundraising, and preparation for the new location's opening.

Adding this campus to The Bridge family was genuinely an act of multiplication on God's part. Opening day saw over 150 people in attendance. The community of believers has remained strong, and as they transition into a new facility they continue to grow. They have celebrated dozens of people coming to Christ and many have gone public with their faith by being baptized in water.

It is glorious how God has used this campus and I prayerfully look forward to the thousands, if not hundreds of thousands of lives that will be reached through the growing community of believers there. This spiritual growth is fueled by the prayer and giving that God has allowed to compound. And that return on equity I was talking about earlier. The people in Bricktown and at the parent location in Mustang are experiencing it!

God has allowed the harvest to multiply for yet a third time as His workers rejoice in the incredible result of their combined prayer and sacrificial giving. When we give our time, talents, and treasures to God, He can and will use our resources for His glory and purpose. This is what scripture means when it says,

> *"Do not store up for yourselves treasures*
> *on earth, where moths and vermin*
> *destroy, and where thieves break in*
> *and steal. But store up for yourselves*
> *treasures in heaven, where moths and*
> *vermin do not destroy and where thieves*
> *do not break in and steal. For where your*
> *treasure is, there your heart will be also."* [1]

SOWING EXPONENTIALLY

Looking forward to the future of God's kingdom creates excitement. Just as we can look at all He has done through us, as His church, we can depend on His promises to keep delivering dividends on the equity to draw upon. God and His plans are beyond our imagining, but we can live our lives sowing seeds and believing in His miraculous power. The power to touch everything within His plan and grow it for His glory.

Being God's children means we share the same promises from Him as the heroes of old in the Bible. We can look to their triumphs to inform and strengthen our faith. Abraham's seed began with Isaac and grew over time into a mighty nation of people more numerous than the stars and greater than the grains of sand on the earth. So, what does that mean for us? How can we live an *unthinkable* life, one with an exponential impact? We need to be a seed planter.

But what does the daily life of a seed planter look like, day-to-day, and how can we make the most of the time God has for us here on the Earth? The life of Jesus was marked by His great compassion, and by reflecting on that we learn one of the greatest seeds to plant is love. Love grows and spreads faster than anything else. When we show God's love to others it is as if we plant a seed in their hearts, in soil made fertile where incredible things are destined to grow. So how do we do that? Make someone else's success your goal.

Scott Wilson, the Global Pastor of the Oaks Church in Red Oak, Texas shared this story, now a favorite. One evening, Scott dreamt of speaking to a crowd of people. As he preached the Gospel, the people rallied and connected with God's message, and their hearts were turning to Jesus. The crowd began to move as he called them to the altar. Suddenly glancing down, the floor of the stage was gone. Everyone else saw Scott standing at the pulpit preaching like normal, but he noticed that he was hovering over a black hole in the floor. Looking even closer, Scott realized that he was standing on his father's shoulders. With tears streaming down his face, his father was praying for him holding him up as he preached supporting him both physically and spiritually.

Who is it that we are called to lift in prayer, and whose feet are we meant to stabilize and secure? God calls us to be a community of believers because we are not meant to serve Him alone. When we seek to edify other believers, God can use us for a greater purpose than we could achieve by ourselves. When you decide to make this life about someone else's successes rather than your own, the world will find that **unthinkable**.

My friend and pastor, Jim McNabb, once said, "Life is so much more fun when you can create a platform that someone else can stand on." He is right. In doing that for me, he fostered a love for helping others that informs everything I do. Since I began my first position in ministry in 2002, I have been privileged to have many spiritual sons and daughters. I have profoundly looked on as many have found success in both life and ministry. I say this to remind us that you teach what you know, but you will always reproduce who you are! Are you merely teaching others addition or are you pointing them to the process of multiplication in their spiritual lives? What are they learning from you?

Leading others to exponential living sounds like a call for teachers, and in some ways it is. Not everyone is a natural teacher, but we can all impact the lives of those around us with God's help. To point others towards God and show them how to navigate through faith could be a heavy burden, but with God, it does not have to be. In his book *Hero Maker*, author and pastor Dave Ferguson talks about how having an exponential mindset takes a willingness to move from being successful to becoming significant.[2] If we want to have an exponential impact with our lives then we cannot remain concerned with simple addition through building our own platforms and legacies. Instead, we need to be focused on the multiplication that comes as we raise others up to do what God has called them to do.

WE NEED TO BE SEED PLANT ERS

Everyone, including me, wants to feel that their life has meaning. As we age, the trivial pursuits of youth fade and the idea of leaving a legacy that endures becomes a salient call in our lives, salting our actions and curating our choices. Perhaps I am late to the game, but recently, my thoughts have centered on how my life of service to Christ has impacted His kingdom. The idea of legacy has become a silent partner in my every day, a wandering thought that has slowly grown to matter more to me than earlier in life.

Since April of 2016, I have had the privilege of serving on the Church Multiplication Network team. They have trained and invested in thousands of church planters since its inception in 2008. In addition to events we host, twice each year we meet, pray, talk, and strategize about how to raise up people to plant life-giving churches in the United States. Our mission is to see a healthy church in every community, and we have a goal to plant 10,000 churches in ten years. Ambitious and *unthinkable*, yes, but when we serve a God that is exponential, we must believe in all His promises. We must take heart in the *unthinkable*, because as God overcomes the world, we see it acted out in our lives each day.

After all, the Great Commission is so big! Jesus calls us in Matthew 28:19 to, "Go into all the world and preach the gospel to every person."[3] Our planet is home to billions of people, and if we are going to reach each one with the Gospel it will take exponential work from all of us to achieve it.

JESUS' EXAMPLE

Jesus was the fulfillment of the plan God had for us. As this chapter, and book comes to a close, let's look to His example. Picture a funnel, wide at the top, and narrowing at the bottom. At the mouth of the funnel sits Jesus, with His complete and perfect love for all humanity. A love unbiased in perfection for everyone equally regardless of human opinion, and who we consider deserving or not. There were many who were outcasts or social pariahs. Zacchaeus, the woman at the well, and the demon-possessed man from Gadara, are just a few examples. He calls us to follow His lead and love others completely as well.

As the funnel narrows slightly, notice Jesus as He lived strategically. The Bible notes that while Jesus loved everyone, He chose His friends carefully. He lived life with the twelve disciples, spent time with them daily, and traveled from place to place together. They were the biblical equivalent of "ride-or-die" friends.

See the funnel narrow to a spout, and here is Jesus, as He led intentionally. Jesus loved everyone, He gave leadership to the twelve, but invested the most into three men: Peter, James, and John.

The Bible does not give us insight into why Jesus chose these men in particular. On many occasions we read about happenings with these three men and nothing about the other nine can be found. Maybe it was because they were the first three to be called, or because they were close friends from their fishing days. Perhaps their hearts were good soil, or it was their zeal and hunger to be around Jesus more than the others. It also could have been a combination of all these things, we are not completely sure. We do know that Jesus invested more in these men than anyone else in scripture. He sought to create reflections of Himself, and it worked.

Peter stood on the day of Pentecost, preached the Gospel, and saw 3,000 people added to the faith that day.[4] He was a key component in starting the New Testament Church as we know it. His eyewitness account may have also been taken into consideration when Mark wrote his gospel.

James, the older brother to John, made an impact for the Gospel with his life as well. He is believed to be the first martyred for his faith by the sword of King Herod Agrippa.[5]

John, the one who lived the longest of all the disciples, wrote five books in the Bible. The last being the Book of Revelation, a prophetic book that looks to the future of humanity and urges us to prepare for the return of Christ.

God used these men in incredible ways because Jesus made strategic investments in them. Thinking about this, how can we apply it to our lives today? If we want to live exponentially, then our relationships should be cultivated as strategically as Jesus's were. Like Jesus, we must love everyone, and we should be selective in whom we invest our time. Choosing friendships and acquaintances knowing that our time will be divided amongst pullers, putters, and pushers, but that our inner circle should be in step with our chosen path. We need to find a small group with whom we share our faith journey and who are going to sharpen us, uplift us, and hone us.

When we prepare to leave a legacy that is exponential, we must wisely invest our best in just a few. So, be choosey, be intentionally strategic and look to find good soil in which to plant your seeds. In full time ministry, this can look like a volunteer leader, staff member, or church planter. As a businessperson, it might be an employee, a shift leader, or store manager. It might be your own son or daughter. My goal has always been for my children to be my greatest disciples.

Regardless of the who, find that person and invest your life in them. To make a difference, we must live differently–and nothing shouts **unthinkable** more than when your life mission is helping someone else succeed. Devote your life to selflessness, imparting significance, and striving for exponential influence in the Kingdom of God.

UNEXPECTED LEGACY

I will never forget moving my family to Oklahoma City in June of 2014. Every weekend and most Wednesdays, I was scheduled to speak at churches across the Midwest to share the vision of what God wanted us to do in Oklahoma City. My weekly routine for the past 14 years changed completely, and I found myself slightly depressed that God's dream for my life was taking longer than expected. Even while we were flooded by God's favor as we traveled to other churches, I began to question if I had heard from God or not. I was discouraged.

Amidst my frustration and gloom, life continued. My grandmother passed in January of that year, and I was unable to attend her funeral in Indiana. Over that summer, my parents came to visit and check out our new city. They brought some belongings of Grandmas they thought I would appreciate, including a Bible passed down from her grandfather.

As I opened the brittle pages, yellowing with age, penned in the top-right corner was:

Charles Wesley Harmon, 1883

Intrigued, I spent time that summer searching Ancestry.com. In between watering the flowers at a local business, doing countless loads of laundry, and even more yardwork, what I discovered blew me away!

All my life I operated under the idea that I was a first-generation minister. As an autoworker, my dad was faithful to General Motors for 38 years and my mother served on staff at a local university. I imagined myself a trail blazer. I believed that I was the only minister in my family, until this Bible came into my life.

Through my research I was able to trace my family line all the way back to a Frenchman named Michael Mauze who founded his hometown. This town, Mauze, still exists today including Chateau de Mauze built by my ancestors. It is a short distance from La Rochelle and is owned by the original Michelin Tire family. I may try to write them and see if I can score a couple night's stay in the old family mansion. (I say jokingly…maybe!)

In the 1500s, the Mauze family were part of a group of protestants known as the Huguenots, later called Quakers. With the population at the time being almost 95% Catholic, the Mauze family left religious persecution in France for freedom in England. After living there for almost 100 years, the family once again set out for religious freedom, and to establish places of worship. This time bound for the New World in America by boat.

My ancestor George Washington Tarvin III was one such Quaker pastor. Some of the very first records kept once colonists arrived talk about descendants from my family playing a key role in the colonies in places like Connecticut, Rhode Island, and Virginia. My family then moved west with the expansion into Kentucky. Leading all the way to my great-great-grandfather, Charles Wesley Harmon, whose Bible came into my possession and who pastored in Indiana.

The genealogy lesson reminds me that God has had a plan for my life long before I was made. As I wrestled with discouragement and feeling alone in my call to church plant and pastor, God showed me that He had been working behind the scenes all along.

I felt the Holy Spirit speak to me about this idea of legacy and He said,

> *"What if you have been thinking that you were chasing God's dream for your life when you have been chasing a dream that reaches all the way back to the 1600's when colonists reached America? What if planting a church in Oklahoma City was the fulfillment of a prayer that someone in your family prayed hundreds of years ago when their ship hit the east coast of the United States? What if the cries of your forefathers were, 'Lord, let our children rise up and take the gospel across the nation'?"*

My ancestors died never knowing that one day my family would land in Oklahoma City! Each year, I have had the privilege to speak in cities across the nation, taking the Gospel in all directions from Tampa to Chicago, San Diego to Washington, DC, and Minneapolis to San Antonio.

When the Holy Spirit said this to me, a part of my heart responded with, *"But Oklahoma is only halfway"*. I shook off this thought and tabled it, justifying it with, *"That's probably for my son or my daughter."* Surely, the Lord was talking about my daughter going to school on the west coast, or my son following his career there one day, right? A part of me questioned, *"What are you saying Lord? We haven't even planted this church in Oklahoma City yet."*

Nearly six years later, a conversation in a rental car on the way to Chicago would forever change my life and bring about the fulfillment of the moment I just described.

In December of 2020, our family said, "Yes" to doing the **unthinkable** once again. We loaded up our home, drove across three mountain ranges in the winter, during a pandemic, to our new home just 40 miles south of Seattle, Washington, to lead and pastor a multi-site church by the name of Newhope.

YOU TEACH WHAT YOU KNOW BUT YOU WILL ALWAYS REPRODUCE WHO YOU ARE!

I am constantly reminded that God does not call us to finish churches, He calls us to start them and to steward them well. Our family never envisioned leaving our church home we started in 2015, but God knew and was preparing me for it all those years ago when my parents gave me my grandmother's weathered Bible. If you would have told me a decade ago where I would be now and what I would be doing, I would have laughed at you, but God knew.

Over the years, God has shown me that we were the answer to lifelong prayers, the fulfillment of someone else's legacy, the embodiment of someone else's prayers! **AND SO ARE YOU!**

The Kingdom of God is immeasurable and the reach of His hand spans across time and space. We all can fulfill the prayer, legacy and hopes of those Christ followers who came before us.

The Challenge is on. If we are going to live the *unthinkable*, then our prayer must be to hear the voice of God. We must forgo the safety of the known and begin doing the hard things. We must forgive easily, give generously, serve sacrificially, and persevere fearlessly. If we seek a world where those around us perceive our actions and lives as *unthinkable*, then we must live daily with our legacy in mind.

Remember, we have everything to gain and nothing to lose – so let us fight the good fight and persevere so our children for generations to come will see the legacy we helped to build. Let us charge into God's *unthinkable* today, so we can see His purpose fulfilled in all our tomorrows.

FIELD NOTES

KEY IDEAS:

- When your goal is to help someone else succeed, the world will find that **unthinkable**.
- You may teach what you know, but you always reproduce who you are.
- An exponential mindset takes a willingness to move from being successful to becoming significant.

FOLLOW-UP QUESTIONS:

1. Who planted seeds in your life? What did they do for you?
2. Describe a time when you impacted someone's life and planted seed. How did you feel?
3. Did the seed you planted in someone else's life have an impact on the person who planted a seed in yours?
4. Who is God calling you to invest in today?

FIELD NOTES

N athan and I have a saying, more of a mantra really, "Don't think about it, just do it. Just do it. Don't think about it, just do it." We say it really fast and then we laugh. Now, God calls us to choose wisdom in all our interactions, but do not let the fear of failure or the plague of indecision bog you down and keep you from completing what God has placed on your heart to accomplish. Do not think so long that it causes you to freeze up. Instead, just do it!

These words might sound familiar because they are the tagline for one of the largest and most recognizable brands in the world: Nike.

Phil Knight, the founder, and owner wrote an inspiring story in his memoir entitled, Shoe Dog.[1] He details the ups and downs of his life: college in the 1960's, his travels in Japan, and the start of his small business that grew throughout the 70's.

He chronicles the relational nuances and different lawsuits he faced over the years. His struggle to overcome and rise to the occasion as he navigated life as a friend, husband, father, and businessman were both sad and inspiring. Through it all, he remained steadfast, his eye on the goal, his fortitude unwavering. He refused to quit. Today, Nike is one of the most remarkable companies this world has ever seen. Take a page out of Phil's book and learn from him, and his slogan. Just do it!

Take what you read in this book and live it out, the time is now. My prayer for you is to go forth, take up the mantle of living out the *unthinkable* and just do it because there is too much at stake to remain unchanged.

Choose the hard things! Spend time in prayer and learn how to hear God's voice in your life. If you forgive easily, give generously, serve sacrificially, and persevere fearlessly, you will leave your mark on the lives of those you touch in ways that will astound you and outlive you. It will look *unthinkable* to the world around you. Not for the sake of your name or your advancement, but to give you a platform so you can point people to Jesus!

Life is a marathon, not a sprint and *unthinkable* living will take consistent daily effort. There are going to be days when you feel like you are accomplishing everything that this book has encouraged you to live out, and days when it feels like you cannot do anything right. So, take it one day at a time.

In the words of the late theologian Eugene Peterson, it is simply a long obedience in the same direction. Sometimes I think we over value what we can do in the short term, and we undervalue what we can accomplish over a longer period of time. Never underestimate what faithfulness can do!

Again, I want to thank you for your time in reading this book and I hope you feel it was a worthwhile investment in your walk with the Lord. The email address at the end of this book is there so you can share your stories with me, as you have allowed me to share with you. I would be honored if you would take the time to write to me and tell how God is using you to live out the *unthinkable* right where you are, in your family, in your church, at your job, and in your community. I love you and I'm proud of you. I believe in you.

You've got this!

-RODNEY

SCAN THE QR OR FEEL FREE TO EMAIL ME AT:

Rodney@unthinkableleaders.com

LET US
CHARGE INTO
GOD'S
UNTHINKABLE
TODAY,
SO WE CAN
SEE HIS
PURPOSE
FULFILLED
IN ALL
OF OUR

TOMORROWS

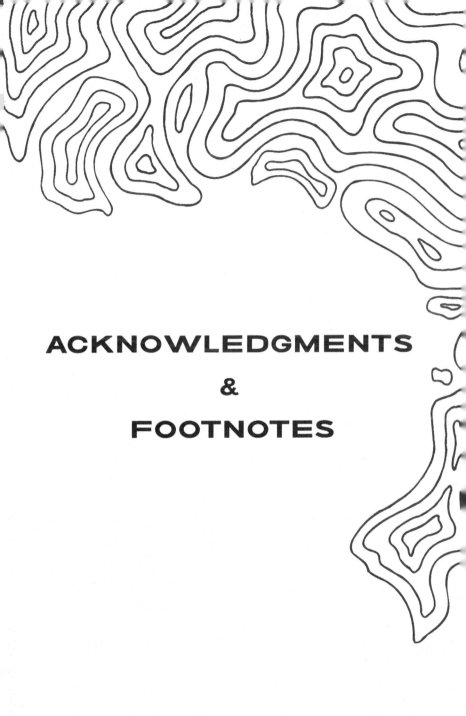

ACKNOWLEDGMENTS

&

FOOTNOTES

ACKNOWLEDGMENTS

There are so many people who gave their time and energy to making a project like this happen. I want to take a minute to say thank you to those on the front lines of this *UNTHINKABLE* movement!

TO MY AMAZING WIFE, KATE

Thank you for supporting me in writing this book. There were many hours at home in front of the computer and many hours reading and re-reading paragraphs to you. Thank you for believing in my dream.

THANKS TO KINDRED CREATIVE

For an incredible book cover, website, and help with marketing.

TO EMILY SMITH

For the book layout work and helping me get this baby published.

TO CRISTINA MILLER

For your help with the editing process.

THE BOOK LAUNCH TEAM

To all of those who served and participated, I'm forever grateful for you.

TO THE PASTORS WHO EARLY ADOPTED *UNTHINKABLE*

And all of the resources we created to start this movement. Thank you for believing in this message and sharing it with others!

TO SOME AMAZING CHURCH FAMILIES

Who have inspired many of the stories in this book from '07 to the current day. I love you and it has been an honor to serve you:

CENTRAL ASSEMBLY
In Enid, Oklahoma

THE BRIDGE
In Oklahoma City, Oklahoma

NEWHOPE CHURCH
In Tacoma, Washington

ACKNOWLEDGMENTS

TO MY FRIENDS AND MENTORS
Who endorsed this message at the front of the book.

TO MY SPIRITUAL FATHER, L. KEVIN WARD
Much of who I am as a pastor, I learned from you. I love you friend. Batman and Robin!

TO MY PASTOR, THE LEGENDARY JIM MCNABB
What an example you are and have been! Thank you for living out the words of this book with your life.

TO JEFFERY PORTMANN
Thank you for entrusting Kate and I with the dream that God gave you and Joanne on that napkin all of those years ago. We are standing on your very broad shoulders. I love you my friend. IGYB!

TO YOU THE READER
The one who is on the journey to do the *unthinkable* with your life, thank you for reading this book. I worked long hours to bring you this message, you don't know how much it means to me that you read it. Now go live it! I believe in you!!

FOOTNOTES

Introduction
1. Ephesians 3:20
2. Ephesians 3:20, NLT
3. Wikipedia, s.v. "Zacchaeus (song)" last modified May 25, 2021, 13:02, en.m.wikipedia.org/wiki/Special:History/Zacchaeus_(song)
4. Luke 19:1-10

Chapter One: Do Hard Things
1. "30 Powerful Thomas Jefferson Quotes on Life, Liberty, and Tyranny," Inspiration Feed, inspirationfeed.com/thomas-jefferson-quotes

Chapter Two: The Underdog Mindset
1. Mark 2:1-12
2. Wikipedia, s.v. "Evan O'Neill Kane," last modified August 6th, 2021, 14:47, en.wikipedia.org/wiki/Evan_O%27Neill_Kane.
3. 2 Timothy 1:7, NLT
4. "John W. Gardner Quotes," Goodreads, goodreads.com/author/quotes/19500066.John_W_Gardner
5. Youtube, s.v. "Don't Stop on Six," 2014. youtube.com/watch?v=g0EO8kr6M8Q
6. Joshua 6
7. 2 Kings 5:14
8. John 2:1-11
9. Google, s.v. "Reed or Rock?" spiritinsport.org.uk/reed-or-rock-lookout/
10. Matthew 16:18
11. Google, s.v. "Reed or Rock?" spiritinsport.org.uk/reed-or-rock-lookout/
12. Acts 2

Chapter Three: Getting to the Spot
1. 1 Timothy 2:8
2. "David Livingstone: Missionary Explorer," Wholesome Words, wholesomewords.org/missions/bliving10.html.
3. Josh Mayo, The Dare, (Youth Leader's Coach, Atlanta, Georgia, 2010)
4. Quote Fancy, s.v. "Smith Wigglesworth Quotes," quotefancy.com/quote/908347/Smith-Wigglesworth-I-don-t-often-spend-more-than-half-an-hour-in-prayer-at-one-time-but-I
5. Wikipedia, s.v. "Honi HaMe'agel," last modified April 28,2021, 18:20, en.wikipedia.org/wiki/Honi_HaMe%27agel
6. 1 Samuel 3:9
7. 2 Kings 6:17

Chapter Four: Forgive Easily
1. Ephesians 4:32
2. Numbers 14:28-29
3. Peter Haas, Broken Escalators. (Salubris Resources Springfield, Missouri, 2015), 116
4. Matthew 18:23-35
5. Matthew 18:33
6. Matthew 18:35
7. Matthew 16:14-15
8. Jeanne Mayo, Jeanneisms. (Youth Leader's Coach, Atlanta, Georgia, 2011) 63
9. Romans 5:8
10. Luke 19:8
11. Luke 19:9

Chapter Five: Give Generously
1. Malachi 3:10-11
2. Genesis 41:39-40
3. Hebrews 11:6
4. Psalm 127:3
5. John 6:9
6. Exodus 16
7. 1 Kings 17:2-16
8. Ephesians 5:15-16
9. 1 Corinthians 12:7
10. 2 Kings 4:1-7
11. 2 Kings 4:3-4

FOOTNOTES

12. John 3:30
13. Luke 6:38
14. "Investment Fail: Why Apple's little-known third co-founder sold his 10% stake for $800," CNBC, cnbc.com/2017/09/12/apples-third-co-founder-ronald-wayne-sold-his-stake-for-800.html

Chapter Six: Serve Selflessly
1. Mark 9:35
2. John 13:1-17
3. Matthew 5:41
4. Matthew 9
5. Mark 2:1-12
6. Exodus 21:24
7. Romans 10:14
8. Matthew 28:19-20

Chapter Seven: Persevere Fearlessly
1. Outreach Magazine, "William Borden: A Life Without Regret," outreachmagazine.com/features/discipleship/31313-william-borden-life-without-regret.html
2. John Wesley, Goodreads. goodreads.com/quotes/626960-light-yourself-on-fire-with-passion-and-people-will-come
3. Educalingo, s.v. "mediocre," educalingo.com/en/dic-en/mediocre
4. Philippians 3:12-14
5. James 1:5
6. 1 Peter 5:8
7. "How Failure Taught Edison to Repeatedly Innovate," Forbes, forbes.com/sites/nathanfurr/2011/06/09/how-failure-taught-edison-to-repeatedly-innovate/?sh=696fb83965e9
8. Brainy Quotes, s.v. "Thomas Edison," brainyquote.com/quote/thomas_a_edison_109004
9. Proverbs 13:20
10. 2 Corinthians 6:14
11. Proverbs 17:7

Chapter Eight: Leave Your Mark
1. NPR, s.v. "Clif Bar: Gary Erickson," npr.org/2018/02/06/572560919/clif-bar-gary-erickson
2. Merriam-Webster, s.v. "Epoch," merriam-webster.com/dictionary/epoch
3. Center for Mark Twain Studies, marktwainstudies.com/the-apocryphal-twain-the-two-most-important-days-of-your-life/
4. Center for Bibliographical Studies and Research, Lompoc Journal, Number 34, 7 January 1911, "Petrified Woman in Pompeii Laden with Real Gems," cdnc.ucr.edu/cgi-bin/cdnc?a=d&d=LJ19110107.2.33&e
5. Brainy Quote, s.v. "Jim Elliot," brainyquote.com/quote/jim_elliot_189244
6. "Charles Haddon Spurgeon Quotes", Goodreads, goodreads.com/quotes/121290-a-good-character-is-the-best-tombstone-those-who-loved
7. 2 Corinthians 3:2-3
8. YouTube, s.v. "Blessed Sons and Daughters – Blessed Families," youtube.com/watch?v=EW5VPnuw44o
9. John 16:33

Chapter Nine: Live Exponentially
1. Matthew 6:19-21
2. Dave Ferguson, Hero Maker. (Zondervan, Grand Rapids, Michigan, 2018.)
3. Matthew 28:19-20
4. Acts 2:14-47
5. "Meet the Apostle James: First to Die for Jesus," Learn Religions, learnreligions.com/profile-of-apostle-james-701062

Conclusion: Just Do It
1. Phil Knight, Shoe Dog. Simon and Shuster, April 26, 2016

IT
IS
TIME
TO
BEGIN
LIVING
THE
UN
THINK
ABLE

THE ~~END~~ BEGINNING